"Nista's book is a burst of light o̲ ̲ ̲ ̲ ̲ ̲ too often complicated by doubt, anxiety or ignorance. And for anyone interested in experiencing freer, deeper pleasure in sex, she is the perfect guide – joyous, highly knowledgeable, compassionate and fun."

— Philip Shepherd, embodiment expert and author of *New Self New World*

"This book is a must-read for anyone interested in conscious sexuality. With raw honesty and without holding anything back, Helena outlines her journey of sexual healing, providing countless tips and exercises to help others do the same. This book will be an amazing resource for people new to tantra, as well as experienced practitioners and therapists."

— Dr Richard Chambers, Clinical Psychologist & Mindfulness Expert

"*Legendary Lover* is moving, eloquent, courageous, insightful and inspiring, and skilfully blends personal experience and practical wisdom with clarity, subtlety and warmth."

— Graeme Piercy, clinical psychologist and sex therapist

"This book is a touching and enlightening journey of a courageous woman's path to sexual awakening. Relatable and timely, Nista reveals candid insights from her direct experience, and offers valuable practices for curious seekers."

— Stephanie Phillips, conscious sexuality coach

"Helena holds space gently and with confidence, and has a versatile range of approaches to draw from. In the work that I have done with her she has proved knowledgeable, professional and in high integrity – qualities that are so important in this field."

— Austin in Melbourne, client

Legendary Lover

6 Essential Steps to Having Great Sex

HELENA NISTA

INDEPENDENT INK

Published 2017 by Independent Ink
PO Box 1638, Carindale
Queensland 4152 Australia

Cover design by Alissa Dinallo
Typeset in 11/16 pt Dante by Post Pre-press Group, Brisbane

Cataloguing-in-Publication data is available from the National Library of Australia

ISBN 978 0 9954 1941 4 (pbk)
ISBN 978 0 9954 1945 2 (mobi)
ISBN 978 0 9954 1946 9 (epub)

TABLE OF CONTENTS

INTRODUCTION

This book was written for men; however, it is also a great resource for women who wish to understand men better sexually and who want to enrich their own sexual experience. I wrote it from my own female perspective and the examples I describe here come from my own life. This is why I keep referring to men and women. However, the techniques, tools and skills I am teaching here are equally applicable to people who identify as gender fluid and who subscribe to any form of sexual orientation. If the male/female dynamic does not apply to you, please feel free to replace these terms with masculine/feminine energy or even active/receptive partners.

The book is based on my experience with my partners, lovers and my sessions with clients. In my pursuit to understand sex and to understand men, I spent countless hours studying men, teaching them, listening to them and making love to them. Over the last three years, I have coached over a thousand clients, teaching them how to be masterful lovers and listening to their feedback and experiences. I have also gone to extreme lengths to educate myself about the art of sex while practicing everything that I was learning about. But aside from all the books, videos, trainings and workshops I was attending, my lovers and my clients were my best teachers, opening up to me about their struggles, challenges and aspirations as lovers.

From my years of practice and experience, I created a unique methodology called LEGEND. This acronym stands for six essential steps to having great sex:

Learn your erotic profile

Engage body and breath

Get off mindfully

Enjoy receiving

Nurture your partner

Discover your full orgasmic potential

This book is divided into six parts and each part tackles one step of my methodology. You will first read about my own experience with a particular practice and then I will introduce you to the theory behind it. I am also including a number of tools and exercises that will help you use everything that you will learn about in this book in your own life.

As you are about to learn, I have been on quite a sexual journey. I started out completely shut down sexually, not enjoying sex, not really knowing how to derive any pleasure and satisfaction from it and really struggling as a lover. This will give you a great insight into the women in your life and how they might be experiencing sex.

Through years of exploration, learning and healing myself, I became multi-orgasmic and deeply connected to my erotic self. My journey will give you insights into what great sex really means, how to have it, how to experience deeply ecstatic states of expanded, orgasmic pleasure and how to help your partner become her most ecstatic self while she is in your arms.

Enjoy the ride!

Part 1

LEARN YOUR EROTIC PROFILE

"He who knows others is wise;
he who knows himself is enlightened."

— Lao Tzu

FRENCH ENCOUNTER

My own scream woke me up in the middle of the night. I had no idea why I was screaming. I started screaming before I was even awake.

I was on an island in France, working as a babysitter for a French family during my summer holidays. They put me in a space adjacent to the garage since there was no spare room in the house. It was dark, very late and no one could hear me scream.

I realized that there was someone in my room. Half-awake, I wondered if I had slept in for my morning duties and reached out for my big, chunky alarm clock. The clock was promptly taken out of my hand as the attacker likely feared that I would use it as a weapon. I tried to turn the light on but the switch did not work and I later learnt that he unplugged my lamp.

In complete darkness, he started to remove my blanket and touch my skin. I kept pushing him away, asking him to leave me alone. I felt a cold, metallic item being pushed against my arm as the attacker advised me to calm down or else. I am still not certain whether it was the fact of being only partly awake or my strong self-preservation instinct kicking in, but I did not stop fighting for a moment. Only later did it occur to me that he most likely had a knife and that I could have been seriously hurt that night.

As I kept pushing his hands away, I kept pleading with him that I was having my period and that he was hurting me. I was terrified and unable to clearly analyse the situation I was in, but I kept doing whatever I could to get out of it.

I guess I was fortunate enough that he was not a cold-blooded monster and when his hand encountered a thick sanitary towel between my legs, he seemed to become hesitant.

After about fifteen minutes, in the face of my stubborn resistance, he finally left my room, leaving me shaking, in shock. The whole thing did not last long but it felt like an eternity. I felt violated, vulnerable and hurt but unable to cry until a few days later, when I reported the whole thing to one of my sisters on the phone.

Why was someone capable of hurting me in order to get sex? What was that all about? Were all men ready for anything in the face of sexual desire? At eighteen years old and still a virgin, I had no answers to these questions.

Early conditioning

Our earliest sexual experiences have a strong influence on our adult intimate lives. Particularly, any strong or traumatic events can leave their mark on our minds and bodies. Even if we do not remember consciously what happened, the memory might be held for many years through muscle tension or involuntary reactions. As we grow older we might or might not question these reactions to particular situations, people or events. Why do I get scared in certain kinds of places?

Why do I automatically distrust certain people? Why do I not enjoy a particular kind of touch? Etc.

Understanding our responses is an important step in building an understanding and awareness of our bodies, hearts and minds. Every time we react emotionally to an event, the body goes through actual physical changes – tension might be created, heart rate might increase, breathing might speed up, hormones might be released and neuro-transmitters or other substances might flood our system. This creates a very real, physical reaction in our system – a reaction which might become hardwired into our being, remaining outside of any conscious control. Do you remember feeling short of breath before an important presentation? Experiencing a wave of shivers when touched by a new lover? Or a painful tension in your stomach upon hearing upsetting news? These sensations are our bodies talking to us, and they are not problematic in themselves unless a reaction starts to affect our lives in a negative way, while we are not able to consciously control it.

Where I grew up, kissing women on the hand is a sign of affection and respect. As a teenager I highly detested this tradition; it felt too invasive for me and my body was creating a storm of refusal within me. As men from my extended family would press their lips to my skin, their wet kisses were creating a wave of discomfort and disgust within me. This reaction is hardwired into my system which is why after all these years I still cringe at the idea of being kissed on the hand by anybody other than my lover. The sheer thought of such contact sends a wave of unpleasant creeps through my chest and arms.

Modern psychotherapy is now recognizing that it is not so much the story that matters in any therapeutic process but the physical reaction imprinted in the body. The story is usually recalled mainly to identify the emotions or reactions our body is still holding in response to the story. Revisiting the story regularly (if it is consciously remembered) is not going to be hugely helpful; it might even re-traumatize the person, or the memory might become a dearly cherished part of our life – after all, we have survived something very upsetting and others should praise us for it.

What needs healing is the energetic mark, the muscle memory that the event left in our bodies. In many cases a strong emotion arose and we were not able to express it properly – shock, fear, frustration, anger, guilt, grief, disappointment ... Our society teaches us that these emotions are wrong and should not be expressed. As a result, we shove our 'negative' emotions down our throats and deny them a healthy expression. This might work in the short run, but in the long term things will eventually blow up, usually when we least expect it. As our stress keeps adding up over the years, remaining calm and balanced will become as tricky as trying to hold a beach ball under water – it will eventually slip out and when it does, this will happen with a spectacular noise and outburst of energy.

Many people in our society have been abused sexually as children. Every time I come across a childhood abuse survivor in my practice, it blows my mind just how much trauma, pain and suffering these people carry or have carried in their bodies. An abusive, invasive touch from an adult hurts deeply. But a conscious therapeutic touch is extremely healing, which is why I am so deeply committed to the somatic practice in my approach. Applying a caring touch, free from agenda or need, can draw out tension and pain created previously, allowing the client to finally process, in a safe and healthy way, what was stuck in their bodies for so many years.

Exercise:

Think back about your childhood and early years of adulthood. Do you recall any events that felt off? Do you feel that your body was violated through uninvited touch? Did you have to hug and kiss all the adults in the family, regardless how you felt about it? Were you slapped as a child? Or did you keep getting rejected when looking for touch and closeness?

How have these experiences affected your current relationship with touch and pleasure? How good are you with intimacy and commitment to a significant other? Are your romantic relationships full of nurturing touch and mutually satisfying lovemaking? Or is touch scarce or one-directional only?

RELIGIOUS HOUSEHOLD

I was raised in a devoted Catholic family in Poland. We went to church every Sunday, to confession every month plus we were always actively involved in different church activities. I was raised to see my body as impure, flawed and not to be enjoyed. The possibility of ever being naked with a man terrified me as a little girl, and I did not discover masturbation until I had my first boyfriend at university.

I cannot even remember any specific messages that I was fed as a child about the body and sexuality. I simply grew up with a strong conviction that the body was sinful, touching yourself was wrong and that pre-marital sex would send you straight to hell.

My parents never talked to us about sex and I suspect that their tension and discomfort around this subject instilled the message in us more strongly than their words ever could. After all, how terrible must this sex thing have been if everybody refused to even mention it?

While attending one of many tantric workshops during the period of my sexual awakening, I was asked about my first self-pleasuring experience. After giving it some thought, I realized that my sexuality was so strongly repressed that, apart from hygienic reasons, I did not even dare to touch my genitals when I was growing up. Instead, I derived an immense pleasure out of repeatedly squeezing my pelvic floor muscle which I seldom indulged in, as it was always accompanied by overwhelming guilt and shame.

This is also when my first sexual fantasies started to form. And without fail, they always involved me being tied up and pleasured against my will. I cannot even express how tortured I felt by them as a child. They were so fascinating to my young mind, so tantalizing, so addictive. And yet so very wrong! I could barely cope with that inner conflict. The only way out that my subconscious mind was able to find was making sure that any sexual pleasure always happened in a rape scenario. Surely you could not be blamed for being pleasured against your will? But I suffered debilitating shame nonetheless.

Sex and parenting

Many people in our society are initiated into the sexual aspect of themselves amidst immense shame and guilt. As soon as we discover that different body parts can be a source of pleasure, we are told to cover up or to stop touching ourselves. The adults feel uncomfortable with a notion that their child might be a sexual being and do not know how to cope with it in a healthy way. And just as they were once shamed and told off by their own parents, they keep repeating the same behaviour with their kids and the cycle of madness and repression continues.

The message we are sending to our children during this process is 'your body is bad, nudity is shameful and pleasure is so, so wrong'.

Girls learn early to keep their legs together and to suppress any desire for a sensual expression. Boys, in the middle of a hormonal storm, find themselves pushed into hiding while seeking self-touch and a genital release. The fear of being caught can be so strong that many young men push themselves to ejaculate quickly, which begins to condition the body towards premature ejaculation.

For many young men, erections are a source of shame and embarrassment. As boys they have to hide any sign of an erect penis, otherwise they might become a target of jokes, teasing or cruelty. Instead of experiencing their sexuality with empowerment and pride, it is a source of guilt and shame.

Even if they did cherish and delight in their sexuality at home, as soon as they were out dating a girl, they had to act as a good boy, completely devoid of their erotic nature, otherwise the girl's dad would never allow any contact between the two.

These young men eventually grow up and become dads themselves, now repressed by the need to act the part in their own family. The desire to be a good husband and father can also carry a lot of repression. As the wife places her attention on the children, their sex life suffers and connecting with other women is not a valid option in our society as it is perceived as wrong, as cheating.

'Masculinity training'

The majority of boys in our society go through a 'masculinity training'. Any aspects of themselves that might be seen as remotely feminine are shamed and rejected. They are told that boys do not cry, that they need to man up and not act like a girl, stripping them of their feelings or of a healthy ability to express them. The only emotions men are allowed to have are strong and negative, like anger.

But the repression is not only emotional. It is also very much about the way they carry themselves in our society; about how they walk, how they move and use their bodies. This is why so many men suffer from tension in their anuses and permanently locked pelvises. Swaying hips are seen as way too feminine. A relaxed anus, open to touch and pleasure, would certainly mean that they are gay and this would expose them to bullying and aggression from their peers. As a society we need so much more healing and education!

Whenever I work on a man's anus, my clients comment with utter surprise about just how relaxing and pleasurable it feels. Well, I bet it feels good when you finally let go of tension you were holding there your entire life! Besides, the anus is one of the most sensitive places in the body which gives it an enormous potential for both pain and pleasure. And guess what – not only homosexual men have sensitive anuses, we all do! But we will come back to that in Part 3.

R. Louis Schultz, PhD writes in *Out in the open, The Complete Male Pelvis*: "Messages, verbal and nonverbal, establish confusing attitudes about the genitals and the anus. How can something that feels so pleasurable be regarded in such a negative fashion? This sets up a pattern that the feeling of pleasure is wrong. (...) The unconscious method of shutting off feelings in the pelvis (or the body in general) is to block the breath into that area. The abdominal breath response will reach down as far as the middle abdomen, while the area of the pubic region will remain very quiet and unresponsive to the breath. This habit no doubt starts in men as babies and is reinforced during growth and development stages. It can be accompanied by the tight anal canal and the pulling in of the penis."[1]

All this suppression seems perfectly normal in our Western society, but it is not the case everywhere. There are tribes and cultures where sexuality is or used to be revered and celebrated. Where young people were initiated into adulthood with full respect of their erotic selves. Where older family members were a source of wisdom and insight about sex and pleasure. Can you for a moment imagine what your life would be like if you were raised this way?

There are lucky individuals who grow up in sex-positive households. But even they will be, to a different extent, affected by the society at large and its conditioning. And our society is plagued by sexual repression. Religious and political institutions do their best to keep us disconnected from our bodies and in denial of our sexual nature. This way it is much easier to control us and keep us tamed. It is also much easier to sell to us, which is why sex is so widely used in marketing. A sexy woman holding a beer, a passionate kiss following a spray of a perfume … We buy an illusion of sex; we buy into the idea that these products will give us back our sexual selves. But nothing external will ever do that for us. The only way forward is to reconnect to our erotic aspect within.

One of the biggest messages I try to instil in my clients is that sex is beautiful and natural and so, so healthy. It is such a vital aspect of who we are that without sex, there would be no humans!

And finally, it is one of the most miraculous and magical ways to express romantic love between partners.

THE END OF INNOCENCE

Not surprisingly, I did not lose my virginity until I was twenty. And my first boyfriend kept raping me for most of the two year period we were together.

We met soon after I started my university degree. We both lived in student houses, about five minutes' walk from each other. Ben was my age and a bit like my dad – an IT specialist, withdrawn emotionally, aloof and smart. Soon he also turned out to be a bully and an aggressive tyrant. After I finally broke up with him, I knew that I would never again allow any man to lay his hand on me.

But at twenty, I was young, naïve and in love.

We waited two months before we had sex. It finally happened at his parents' place in the mountains and the whole act consisted of him forcing his penis inside me, moving in and out a bit and then ejaculating. It was painful, uncomfortable and stressful as it happened in the middle of the day and his parents were in the next room. I was certain we would get caught and I was freaking out about it.

They say you never forget your first time. But I always imagined it would have been for good reasons …

He also introduced me to oral sex which felt really good. But I was not allowed to enjoy it too much as he kept getting more and more forceful waiting for me to orgasm. Unfortunately, at that time I had no idea that you could fake a climax so my poor clitoris suffered a lot of rough treatment. His manliness was strongly attached to his performance as a lover so I had to orgasm, whether I liked it or not.

So I did my best to orgasm every time. I was squeezing my legs and my pelvic area. I was concentrating as hard as I could. And then finally I would manage to squeeze out an orgasm – a brief release, hardly pleasurable, hardly worth it. I would have been perfectly happy without it.

There was no point asking him to stop, he would never listen. And I had never learnt that I had a say when it came to my body, that my 'no' could be respected. My body belonged to my partner so he could do with it as he pleased. Nobody ever told me that my body was sacred, that it was a gift, that I had a right to protect it from pain and abuse.

Looking back, I cannot believe that I did not experience arousal for so many years. I sure as hell never felt aroused with Ben, which did bother me a little. I knew from movies that some people felt this heated urge to merge physically; they just had to be together sexually to the point of ripping each other's clothes off and giving in to their urges right there and then, as soon as they walked in the door, on the stairs leading up as they usually did not even make it to the bedroom.

I never felt like ripping anybody's clothes off. I never looked forward to sex. It was a duty, a part of being in a relationship. So I kept fulfilling my duty, as often as my partner wanted me to. Regardless of how I felt about it.

So many times I lay in his bed, with him on top of me, my entire body shaking in pain while he was penetrating me, tears pouring down my face as I was begging him to stop. He never did until he was done.

Back then I did not know that I was being raped. I had no idea that I could get help. I was clueless about who I could speak to, so I kept quiet.

I was learning that sex meant penetration alone, that it was about fast thrusts in a chase towards his orgasm and that as soon as it was over, I needed to clean myself quickly in order to remove the excess sperm from my vagina, otherwise it would leak out onto the sheets.

Ben also forced me to start shaving my intimate area, so once again I was learning that my body was not perfect the way it was and that 'natural' meant 'flawed'.

Porn-based sexual education

I was getting a first-hand experience of a sex education based on porn. Whether coming from printed magazines or the computer screen, the images that sink deep into young brains are full of sex that is fast, furious and disconnected. Women are treated as objects of male desire and pleasure, without minds or opinions of their own. So men learn to take from women instead of nurturing them. To use their bodies instead of connecting with them. And women learn that their genitals should respond with arousal quickly and that they should be capable of orgasming as quickly as men do.

I do not think that there is anything inherently wrong with enjoying sexual imagery as long as it does not distort our understanding of reality. And the reality is that porn-style sex rarely works in our own bedroom. The truth is that women need to relax and surrender in order to reach the depths of their orgasmic potential. They need to feel safe, seen, respected and cherished, instead of the whole sexual act being reduced to being mechanically thrust into for a few minutes. And despite all the focus on rock-hard erections and semen squirting all over her body, what men really deeply crave is to know that they have satisfied their lover and that their woman had a mind-blowing experience. I have not met a man in his right mind who does not care about that. And I have met a lot of men.

But despite this deep rooted desire to satisfy the partner, there is a lot of frustration in bedrooms all over the world. And that is because modern society does not offer a good quality education around good quality sex. I am appalled that to this day all that schools are capable of offering their students is a rushed condom talk delivered by one of the teachers who is visibly uncomfortable with the subject. This does not create a good environment for an honest conversation about consent, boundaries, building intimacy and connection, about arousal, pleasure, touch, orgasms, self-pleasuring or what good sex actually looks like.

In fact I personally welcome every opportunity I get to speak to teenagers about sex. I am absolutely thrilled by the sheer thought of these young people entering the world of sex with a clear vision of what being intimate really means and how to create magical, unforgettable moments with their partners. If you feel that your local school needs me, get in touch!

GIVING UP FAITH

Around that time I finally walked out of church. At that stage paedophilia among clergy was making the news and someone close to me had actually been abused sexually by a priest at the age of eight years old. I was really struggling with the necessity of connecting to God through men who were hurting children.

Didn't God say that he was everywhere, omnipresent, always loving and caring? Church was making less and less sense to me. I was perfectly happy talking to God all by myself. I doubted he would reject me because I refused to address him through the clergy.

Unfortunately, my family felt differently and I was subjected to many attempts at converting me back to Catholicism. I did not give in and so that time in my life was marked by loneliness and rebellion. Estranged from my parents, lonely in my relationship, I found some support in my sisters and friends.

After two years, I finally gave up on Ben and walked out of the relationship. As a result, my entire system experienced a sort of a shock.

I grew really addicted to Ben and he always managed to convince me that I was guilty of any problems between us. My naïve nature was no match for his sharp mind. So I believed that even our painful sex was my fault and, following his advice, I asked my gynaecologist to cut my vagina more open. Thank God the doctor was sane enough to refuse. He examined me, told me that there was nothing physically wrong with me and recommended that I place two fingers inside myself and practice pushing them apart to widen my vaginal canal. I tried it once or twice but the exercise was so uncomfortable that I gave up.

The following year, I was involved with three more men. Fortunately, sex was not as painful as before. But it still was not terribly pleasant either. It seemed to always follow the same scenario – a bit of kissing and fondling, followed by impatient penetration that lasted for a few minutes and culminated in his ejaculation. I was learning to enjoy the furious thrusting inside me despite the pain. I actually learnt that once I pushed through the pain, I could then feel some pleasure. And that is what I kept doing, ignorant of the fact that my body was at this stage so desensitized and numb that only intense friction could make me feel anything. In fact, my genitals started the process of armouring (desensitizing) at the very beginning of my sexual journey, so I really did not know any better. My vagina felt either numb or uncomfortable. A lot of friction allowed me to feel some pleasure but I was still far, far away from having any of the sort of orgasmic moments that I kept witnessing in movies. What did they all do that I did not? What did they know? How were they different than me? I could not figure it out.

Two of these lovers were friends with benefits and the third one I had a serious crush on. After a month together he broke up with me and shattered my fragile heart into a thousand little pieces.

A month later I left Poland.

Developing self-awareness

What I was truly missing in that time of my life was some self-knowledge and familiarity with my body. The truth is that it is extremely hard to be a great lover to your partner if you have not explored your own body all by yourself first. Many women do not touch themselves until much later in life. The societal conditioning around women's sexuality is very negative. If she loves sex, she's a slut, a loose woman not worthy of respect. Many women have never seen their own genitals properly, or another woman's genitals.

For men this situation is quite different. Masculine sexuality is not repressed as strongly and sleeping around is a measure of his success with women. Male genitalia are located mostly externally and are much easier to see and examine than a vagina. Many men have also seen other men naked in public toilets and showers.

Pretty much all men start to masturbate during their teenage years, but with women this varies greatly. Some girls are open enough to start touching and connecting with their own body early on in their lives. But many experience so much shame and repression that they do not start until they are in their 20s or 30s!

Once we do start to touch our bodies, we act without any guidance or advice. We do not have a lot of understanding about our genital anatomy, erectile tissue or about how arousal works and how to get the most out of it for truly mind-blowing orgasms. We develop masturbation routines that do not change much over the years. Just think, do you still masturbate the same way you did ten years ago? You're not alone – many people do!

Exercise:

Next time you connect with your own body, I would like you to invite more mindfulness, more curiosity into your practice. Do not go straight for old, tested strokes. Try new ones. Include your entire body in your practice. Give yourself a loving self-massage! And once you get to your genitals, use your non-dominant hand for a change. Slow down and really notice what your body is feeling. Stay there, do not rush, do not chase that orgasm. Just be in pleasure for the sake of pleasure. Allow the yummy sensations to last. Why would you hurry anyway? Make time for a long, sensual session of self-love. And try to not use fantasy or porn. Simply remain mindful, connected to your body. Experiment. Use props, different textures, reach for coconut oil. Play your body like an instrument. There is no script, nothing to achieve. Touch your own body the way you would touch the body of your beloved – with love, care, kindness, indulging all your senses, taking your time. Enjoy!

SONG OF IRELAND

My move to Ireland was the biggest leap of faith in my life. I spent all the money I had on my airfare and the one hundred euro banknote in my pocket was not going to carry me far if the family I was meant to babysit for did not show up at the airport for me.

But I was excited, happy and tremendously relieved to finally leave my country for good. I could hear the song of Ireland in my heart; it was calling me with the most beautiful, enchanting voice, promising fairies, elves, druids and all sorts of magic.

At twenty-three years old, I felt ready to spread my wings and fly. To explore the new world and to learn as much as I could. I was also extremely curious how Irish men had sex since I had only been with Polish men so far …

I found Irish people extremely welcoming and friendly. The family that I was staying with for the first five months did their best to make me feel welcome. I also got a job in a local bar and soon started meeting a lot of people. It turned out that a young and pretty Polish girl full of smiles was not a very common thing to see in Youghal, a small town of approximately five thousand people. So I quickly started to attract a lot of attention. Not all of it good – men loved me and women hated me or, at best, felt neutral about me. After all, I could take their men away but at the time I did not understand their resentment.

Free to do whatever I pleased, I decided to have fun and enjoy this new world I was in. I did not find love for the first two years but that did not stop me from having sex. I always had at least one lover, but I did not stick with anyone for longer than a few months. I do not recall having any one-night stands – ever. But if I liked someone, the conversation was good and I enjoyed his company, I did not see why we could not have sex.

Sexuality kept fascinating me, but I was still uncertain how I could learn anything new. Access to internet was still very limited back then, plus you would not be able to find a lot there regarding sexual education. So I kept up my hands-on practice, hoping to become a great lover through quantity rather than quality.

To my surprise, sex in Ireland was pretty much the same as sex in Poland. The three-step formula held valid across the borders: 1) foreplay, 2) penetration, 3) ejaculation. Foreplay varied from person to person but never seemed to last too long. There was always a sense of impatience there – the point of the whole exercise was to put the penis inside the vagina, so why waste time on anything else? Once inside, a series of fast thrusts followed but at this stage I learnt to play with different positions, which helped to make it all last a bit longer. But once the penetration started, all my lovers still seemed so distant from me, like they were in their own world of deep pleasure that I was always denied access to. I did my best to enjoy myself but remained anorgasmic for many, many years.

I kept experimenting with masturbation, but was always left with a sense of 'is that all?' afterwards. I loved stroking my clitoris and, when alone, I could bring myself to orgasm within a few minutes. But the peak lasted only a few seconds, and in many cases there did not even seem to be any peak there! Once I brought myself to the point of vaginal contractions, sometimes I felt lovely pleasure in my genitals and in many cases – nothing at all.

So I was touching myself less and less. I was becoming even more disconnected from my body, subconsciously rejecting it because of the frustration I was experiencing.

I was living my life in my head as opposed to in my body. Once I became proficient enough in English, I enrolled in evening courses, I studied computers and accounting. I was determined to move on from babysitting and bar work. My body remained neglected. I did not work out or eat healthy. I was slowly learning about nutritional values, but it all seemed pretty vague to me since I was completely unfamiliar with the 'you are what you eat' concept. Fortunately, I never had any problems with my weight and my body seemed to cope pretty well with my unhealthy habits. Besides, I was getting enough exercise during long hours behind the bar.

After two years in Ireland, I met Sean. He rented a room in a shared house I was staying in, still in Youghal. I am an introvert and an extremely private person so I kept avoiding him as much as I could, but when we finally connected, we became partners immediately. He was such a beautiful soul! Warm, open and funny. After cold and withdrawn Ben, Sean felt like an angel to me and I could not get enough of him.

The concept of delaying gratification was completely foreign to me when it came to sex, so we slept together that very same night we finally spoke at length. And he moved into my room soon after that.

After two years of wild partying and dating, I was tired of that life-style and disillusioned about the depth of my connections. I craved stability and partnership; I wanted to have a home, not just a house. I loved Sean and he loved me, so we soon bought a house together. But things were far from perfect and I had an uneasy feeling that this was not my 'forever story'.

I still remember that first time we had sex. In complete darkness, with no words. I removed my pyjama bottoms as he started to kiss me, and soon he was inside me. I was lying on my back, my top still on while Sean kneeled between my legs and raised my hips in order to enter me. Some nice feelings followed as he was rhythmically thrusting inside me, bumping our genitals and bodies against each other.

I fell asleep in his arms, feeling warm and happy.

Core Erotic Theme

At fifteen years my senior, Sean was the first – but not the only – man in my life who was much older than me. For a reason I did not under-stand at the time, I felt much more attracted to men in their forties and fifties than I was to men of my own age. Guys in their twenties and thirties seemed so immature, did not have much to offer in terms of a good conversation, and I was getting bored with them quickly. Older men were so much more experienced in life, so fascinating, had so many amazing stories and so much wisdom to share!

In fact, what I was experiencing were the effects of my Core Erotic Theme. I was introduced to that concept much later in life while reading *The erotic mind* by Dr. Jack Morin[2]. Your core erotic theme starts to form very early in life when you are learning to relate to the world as a small child. Any significant experiences, confusion, hurt feelings, etc., can contribute to it. Your mind creates this erotic theme in attempt to fix or heal unfinished business from your childhood.

The most common childhood wounds are caused by parents. Many people carry a father-wound of abandonment where the dad was perceived as emotionally or physically distant, often not available for a nurturing touch or a quality time together. We start seeing ourselves as not worthy of love because the parent was not present for us. We start to seek validation through work and career, but the pursuit never ends because the wound goes much deeper and cannot be satisfied by superficial means. The healing needs to address the core issue here – lack of self-worth, fear of rejection and abandonment.

Other people experience a wound caused by the mother if she was smothering us, overly connecting or connecting unlovingly. Women often seek their own validation through their children which can lead us to believe that love and intimacy are not safe. We start to believe that if we love someone, they will take from us and so we subconsciously protect ourselves from such intimate connections.

Some people carry both these wounds.

According to the *Song of Tantra* by Chantelle Boscarello (Raven) and Simon Martin, "if we had Healthy Masculine presence which was available both emotionally and physically, we will be less likely to have a fear of abandonment and rejection. Presence is the gift of the Masculine. If we had Healthy Feminine nurturance which was not dependent on filling a void or meeting the parent's needs, we will be less likely to have fear of intimacy and closeness. Unconditional Love is the gift of the feminine."[3]

Exercise:

You can examine your own core erotic theme by looking into your most exciting, memorable erotic experiences. What do they all have in common? What stands out as a common factor in all these stories? Why were these situations so arousing?

Another way to look into it is by analysing your sexual fantasies. What elements keep repeating in all different scenarios that your mind is creating? What situations, people, places, interactions do you find most arousing and why? Where does your imagination go when you are looking to quickly boost your excitement?

If you watch porn, what kind of sexual imagery do you go for? Who excites you? What are they doing and with whom? Why do you think you choose this particular kind of video?

Unhealthy attractions

At that stage of my life I had never watched porn and could not recall anything even close to a memorable (in a positive sense) erotic experience. All I could go by were my fantasies and attractions I was experiencing in my life.

For many years of my life my sexual fantasies revolved around one theme – rape and sexual abuse. As a child, I remember fantasising about being tied up and teased sexually, but I would never dare to touch myself 'down there'. The church taught me that my intimate parts were dirty and disgusting. I would occasionally squeeze my pelvic floor muscle for more pleasure and sensation, but I did not allow myself to indulge in these fantasies or squeezes too often because of a huge amount of shame and guilt that I felt after. Over the next twenty years, my sexual fantasies remained pretty much the same – always tied up and teased sexually by a group of men that I didn't know. I guess this scenario allowed me to feel less guilt as I surely could not be blamed for being a victim of rape and abuse.

In fact, a rape fantasy is very common among women. This is by no means an indication that these women actually want to be raped. It simply indicates a level of sexual suppression that the mind is experiencing. I do believe that our imagination would create something much more exciting if given a full permission to delight in sex and pleasure.

My attraction to older men was also strongly indicative of my core erotic theme – seeking externally a validation that I had never received from my own dad. A father of six beautiful beings, he never sought an opportunity to connect with us when we were kids. To this day it is a family joke that he never learned to make a braid, despite having five daughters with long lush hair. When he was home, he was on his computer in his bedroom, with the door tightly shut. He even placed a 'danger' sticker on his door in order to keep us away. The sticker was a yellow triangle with an image of a skull and two bones crossed below, the type that you see on high voltage electricity units. I bet not many people were raised in a home with an image of a skull on one of the doors!

As a child I felt abandoned by my father and kept doing all I could to get his attention and approval. My attempts were not successful and so for many years to come I was stuck in a loop of seeking out older men and attempting to get from them the validation and love I was craving. But even when they did love me, the core wound remained un-healed so I kept repeating the pattern again and again, and again.

GREAT EMIGRATION

A routine soon developed between me and Sean and we had sex once or twice a week in the same anonymous way. Once again sex became my duty as a girlfriend and I derived less and less pleasure from it. I remember always having two thoughts on my mind during the act itself: a) he forgot to take his watch off again and it is hurting my skin and, b) as soon as he is finished I will be able to read my book.

I stopped masturbating altogether; after all, I had a boyfriend now so he was meant to attend to my sexual needs. Or that is what I believed. I had no idea that all along I was the person responsible for my own pleasure, for my sex and for my orgasms. I kept placing that responsibility in the hands of my partners, who did not really know much more about sex than I did! So we carried on, empty and unsatisfied.

Sean and I were actually really good friends and we made each other laugh a lot. I believe that humour kept us together for so long because deep down we did not really have too much in common.

Besides, Ireland felt less and less like home to me, so Sean was keeping my spirits up and keeping me from becoming depressed.

Over time he also became increasingly jealous. I was working in an accounting firm at that stage and making some extra money preparing tax returns for a few Polish contractors working nearby. Sean could not understand our language and was convinced that I was cheating on him. This could not have been further from the truth; I was definitely not looking for more sex. Would you really want more sex if it was mostly painful and you never orgasmed? No, neither did I. But I knew that all of Sean's previous partners cheated on him and I was the first faithful one. So it seemed really unfair that I was the one he was pouring his bitterness and disappointment onto, particularly after a bottle of wine. I grew to deeply despise his drinking. He converted one of the bedrooms in the house into a recording studio and was spending long hours there with at least one bottle of wine each time. Any conversation between us in those moments would turn into him complaining about all the women in the world and how much they had hurt him. My comforting words never seemed to help. He was hurting, and so was I while listening to him. I eventually learned to leave the room after about an hour or so, regardless of whether he was done talking or not. These chats always happened late at night and I had to get up at 6am to get to the office. Besides, I felt powerless to help him or make him feel better.

That was when I discovered women. At that time I was chatting a lot to a lesbian friend of mine in Poland and I started to fantasize about being one too. I felt that I was done with men; they did not seem to have anything to offer me. I definitely did not want any more penises inside me.

I decided it was time to leave Ireland and to move to the USA. I definitely needed better weather and larger opportunities for my life.

Ireland with its rolling hills, amazing beaches and deeply green land-scapes is one of the most beautiful places in the world, but it was hard to appreciate its beauty while being constantly stuck indoors due to unfriendly weather. I was also feeling more and more estranged from my Irish friends. All they seemed to want to do was to go to the pub while I wanted growth, progress and self-development. I believe they truly were not certain why I would choose to go to an evening school instead of having a pint with them at a local bar. As I started looking into my American dream, the global financial crisis hit the world and my plan was over before it even began to form.

After searching some more, I set my eyes on Australia. With its great weather and English speaking population, it seemed like an easy enough transition for me. I soon got a job in an accounting firm in Melbourne which was a requirement for an employer-sponsored visa – my only possible way to start a new life down under. And after six months I had a visa and a one way ticket.

Sean was originally meant to come with me, but I felt it would have been unfair to take him along as my partner when our relationship felt over. It was so hard to tell him that I was leaving without him! I still love him dearly and wish him all the best. I did soften the blow by telling him that deep inside I was gay. For the first time ever he admitted that our sex life was not good. His broken heart found some consolation in my sexual confusion.

I sold, gave away or threw out everything I owned. I packed a suit-case full of clothes and left on a thirty-hour journey to the land down under.

PINKALICIOUSNESS

Melbourne turned out to be everything it promised to be and more. Hot, sunny, vibrant and exciting, it was the place to be for me at twenty-seven years old. Once again I was in a new place, wide-eyed, mesmerized and eternally grateful for this new chance in life.

I was keen to start making friends and exploring my newly found lesbian self. I joined an online dating site for women and prepared for the unknown. I had seen some lesbian porn in Ireland, so I had some idea about same-sex couples. I also found it really arousing to watch girls together, which seemed like a good sign.

I finally felt liberated from men and their harsh ways. My body was craving a woman's touch and I was determined to find it. But I was not just after sex, I wanted love. I was absolutely fascinated by the idea of being with a woman. To be with and be touched by someone like me felt like a natural answer to all my previous struggles. I just needed to find her and make her want me as much as I wanted her.

My online dating efforts were not bringing any significant results. I went on a few dates but did not feel any romantic connection with anybody.

I knew that men found me attractive but I had no idea whether I would be attractive in the lesbian world, so I was keen to find out.

Things started to progress a bit more when I discovered the Pinkalicious parties in the city. At a fun venue for women only I felt very comfortable and at home. Women felt safe and gentle, even the butch ones who kept inviting me to their hotel room for some no-strings-attached sex.

It felt so good to dance with girls, to hold their tiny little waists in my hands, to caress their bodies and to be caressed by them. Their bodies felt so different to the men. Women are so fragile, so delicate; they smell and taste so good. Their kisses had none of the forcefulness I had usually experienced with men. There was no impatience, no rush, no agenda. They did not seem to want to get anywhere in a hurry; they were happy to just be together, to touch, kiss, talk, share.

I instinctively knew that this new, lesbian way of being together suited me tremendously and I was ready to find my one and true love in this world. But after six months went by, I was still single and my resolution to be gay started to wane.

At my last Pinkalicious party I noticed a male waiter in the room and realized that I actually missed penis, and that men were not so bad after all. I also figured, rightly or wrongly, that we were all bi-sexual and that true love was between two people connected deeply at the heart and soul level, regardless of the shape of their genitals.

I was still open to women, but it felt easier to go back to the hetero-sexual world in my pursuit of love and sexual satisfaction.

Sex-ploration

Exploration is very healthy and natural. Curiosity can lead us to finding new territory, trying new ways, to experimenting. And as long as there are consenting adults involved, I do not believe that you should be placing any boundaries on your exploration. Would you like to try a threesome? Do sexual toys seem enticing to you? How about a same sex sexual experience? Or even just a kiss with a person of a gender you are not usually attracted to? Or a particular type of sexual images?

During straight sex roles are usually assumed and particular scenarios play out in a very similar way, over and over again. There is not a lot of room for experimentation as men usually prefer to be active and women usually prefer to be passive. So he usually initiates, there is some mutual kissing and fondling of genitals and then penetration follows until he comes.

But just try to imagine sex in a lesbian couple. No roles are assumed (unless a particular couple creates such roles) and nobody is meant to do anything in particular or in any particular order. In my experience, there is much more room for connection and mutual touch and nurturing when both people involved play with roles, becoming either more active or more receptive.

The routine that so quickly develops in male-female intimacy (1/ foreplay, 2/ penetration, 3/ ejaculation) has no room between two women, as the focus on release is not so strong. For many men sex seems to be all about orgasm. I even heard someone ask, 'Why would you even want to have sex if you were not going to orgasm?'. Oh boy, how sad it makes me feel that sex might be viewed in such a narrow way!

Sex is an amazing opportunity for people to connect on a very deep, profound, intimate level. You can have absolutely magical experiences together without one orgasm happening during the interaction.

In fact, many women in our society do not orgasm during sex, and do not allow that to bother them as they receive immense pleasure and satisfaction from the sex act alone.

This is definitely not to say that there is a problem with orgasms. There is not and I absolutely love them! But if your sole goal during sex is to reach an orgasm, you are missing out on tons of experiences along the way.

Exercise:

Next time you connect with your beloved, simply slow down and really notice what you are feeling in your body, moment by moment, touch by touch. Notice all the pleasure, all the surrender in this experience, all the energy travelling deliciously up your chest and head, down your arms and legs, notice your partner and how her body feels next to yours. Savour sex with your entire being; take it in through all of your five senses. Delight in it without any agenda and your capacity to feel ecstatic will expand tremendously.

SUGARLAND

I went back to dating men in their forties and fifties. As opposed to younger men, they had already accomplished a lot and were more interested in life's pleasures and enjoyment than in their careers. They had wealth of experience to share and could mentor me and help me out on my way. They also took me to really nice places and always seemed absolutely delighted with my company.

They wanted threesomes, some wanted to go to gentlemen's clubs with me, some just wanted to go away for a weekend of sex and fun. I was ticking away boxes of sexual experiences like there was no tomorrow while the men were covering all the costs. I liked that freedom, and I was glad to try things that I would have never tried otherwise. It was a time of play, indulgence and enjoyment.

It seemed like a win-win situation. Until we entered the bedroom.

When it came to sex, the same routines held valid for men of all ages. These older men made love in exactly same way as the young ones – in a rushed, disconnected way! This is definitely not to say that all men make love this way. What I am describing here is simply my own experience, not the way things are everywhere or for everybody.

Unfortunately, I did not bring any of my acquired lesbian experience back with me. And when I was with a man, I reverted back to making love like a man, with a focus on his release. This felt to me like the only way to have heterosexual sex. There was nothing else I knew about the penis-in-the-vagina sex. The foreplay was quick or non-existent, and the whole point of the intimacy was for him to ejaculate during penetration.

Gone were the days of a slow, sensual touch; of exploring each other's skin for the sake of feeling pleasure; of finding delight in kissing and caressing without any particular goal in mind.

So I was back in square one, and it never even occurred to me to make or even propose any changes. I felt that all that the men wanted was to come, and the rest was an unnecessary fluff that girls would bug them for.

This life was not satisfying to me, and ultimately I found myself frustrated and lost again. I was craving love and connection, yet I was stuck in a circle of empty encounters, void of deep emotions or a spiritual dimension.

After a year, I finally fell in love again.

Creating a connection

Sex without a deep connection is just a meeting of two bodies, two sets of genitals. It can feel very pleasurable and fun, but ultimately we are left feeling unfulfilled and unmet. Human beings have a profound yearning for an intimate connection that involves more than just the physical realm. We want to merge with a significant other, we want to connect through minds, hearts and souls. And that kind of connection requires more work, more time. It requires trust, surrender and giving yourself to the other completely.

When you open your heart, it creates a new quality within you, a new dimension – that of raw, authentic emotional connection. When two open hearts meet this way, sex becomes much more – it turns into lovemaking.

Exercise:

I teach my clients a very simple practice of opening their hearts with a beloved before they move on to physical lovemaking. I ask them to sit facing each other and to become fully present. Maybe taking a few deep breaths together or even meditating for a few minutes in order to rid the mind of all the distractions of the day. It is very difficult to fully meet your partner when your head is full of thoughts about work, cooking, shopping or worries about kids. So let them all go and bring your entire attention into the room with you.

Next take turns sharing with each other what it is that you love about each other. Let one person start by connecting to their heart and saying the words "I love it when …". It does not matter if you have no idea what to say. Simply feel the love in your heart and the words will flow. "I love it when you smile and kiss me every time I come home from work; in fact, I look forward to that smile on my way home and it warms my heart to know how happy you are to see me." "I loved it when we went for a walk together last night and you held my hand all the way. And when you told me about that time you felt worried about our relationship. I am so grateful that you care so much about our connection." "I love the way you are with our children. You treat them with so much love, care and patience. I am proud to call you my wife."

You can share a few things each, or swap each time one of you shares something. It is your game and you make the rules. Simply make sure to keep your heart open, allow yourself to be very raw, authentic, even vulnerable. There is no true intimacy without vulnerability. Allow your partner to really see your heart, to experience your emotions, to bask in your depth. And then in turn hold your lover's heart with reverence and compassion. Witness her sharing with respect and love. Know that it is a great honour to be let deep inside into another's heart.

REVERSED COWGIRL CRISIS

I met Jacques through a mutual friend who thought that we might be good together. Fourteen years older than me, tall, dark, handsome and French, Jacques was my Prince Charming and soon – the love of my life.

It was a no-brainer to me. I left my previous life behind and became a loving, devoted girlfriend. We were perfect for each other; we had a lot in common, we could talk for hours and he seemed very balanced, grounded, strong and an excellent provider. After just over a year together, I moved in with him and we decided to have a baby together.

I was truly done with dating. All I wanted was to be a wife and a mother, and to be with Jacques for the rest of my life. The sex did not even bother me, I gave up on trying to be someone other than I was sexually, and I accepted sex for what it was. Maybe I was just not meant to have vaginal orgasms, mind-blowing pleasure or transcendental experiences.

Jacques had a very high sex drive and we had sex at least once a day. It always consisted of only penetration and never lasted longer than five minutes. Some days we were done within seconds, which I welcomed with relief.

As much as I could, I would try to avoid penetration by giving him oral sex, but he usually insisted on me taking him inside me, with me always on top so that he did not have to do a lot. At least after the oral, his penis was wet with my saliva so the penetration was gentler on my dry, unaroused vaginal canal.

I had never been with a lazier lover but it was ok with me. It was what it was. I was accepting what I felt unable to change. I was so in love, I would follow him to the end of the Earth anyway. Who cared about great sex? What we had was fun and we were happy.

Jacques' appetite for sex kept growing and he kept requesting three-somes and new sexual positions. I really struggled with the prospect of sharing him with another woman, so we finally made it happen in the safest way possible – we hired an escort during our European trip. There was no risk of an emotional attachment growing between the two of them so I felt safe enough to go through with this experience.

When he asked for a reversed cowgirl position, I had no idea my life was about to change dramatically.

This position in itself is not particularly challenging; however, it does involve a very deep penetration. My vaginal canal is quite short and the penis usually hits my cervix easily. This is part of the reason why sex had always been so painful to me, plus the lack of any vaginal lubrication did not make things any better. I was capable of lubricating but was not doing so, since nobody ever took the time to arouse me properly.

One morning we started off as usual and the reversed cowgirl was once again on the menu. As soon as he ejaculated inside me, I rolled off and lay down on my back to rest for a moment. Jacques was up while I was indulging in a few extra minutes in bed.

Suddenly I felt a wave of anxiety in my body. I had no idea what was happening, but it was not good and I was scared. Trying to figure out the source of my discomfort, I felt my entire body contracting for about ten seconds of excruciating pain and extreme tension. After that the pain eased off but did not go away. I started breathing again and then the next wave of pain gripped my body with an even stronger force. All I could do was to lie there and wait for it to go away, eyes shut tight and completely breathless.

After about five waves of increasing pain, the level of intensity seemed to settle with the pain gripping me for about ten seconds and then easing off slightly for about five. At that stage I knew that this was serious and that it was not going to just go away. The pain was localized in my lower belly and it seemed to have been caused by sex. It was so strong that I was fearing the worst: I was either going to die or I would never be able to have sex again.

Tears in my eyes, I called Jacques and asked him to call an ambulance. Very concerned, he advised me that the ambulance could take an hour to get to us, whereas an emergency room was about five minutes' drive away. I could not move! How was I going to get out of bed, get dressed and drag my sore body all the way to the car?

I gathered my entire strength and finally crawled out onto the floor. On all fours, I slowly made it to my wardrobe and eventually managed to put on some clothes. Jacques helped me out to the car and we left. I think he really appreciated the seriousness of the situation when he saw my face convulsed in extreme pain again and again, and again.

I still do not know how I managed to walk into the hospital all by myself, while Jacques was parking the car. My pelvis kept exploding in pain and my legs were stiff from the tension. All I could concentrate on was making sure that I kept moving forward – one painful step at a time.

Inside, I was asked to sit down and wait. At about 6.30 am, there were only a few other patients around. I was ready to kill the staff for keeping me there for what felt like an eternity. I was so close to getting help, yet I had to sit, wait and endure.

After about fifteen minutes I was finally lying on the hospital bed with someone attending to me. After a short examination, I was informed that the pain was coming from my bladder. It seemed that I was very dehydrated. I did not understand how this could send me into such a torture until another piece of the puzzle became obvious.

Jacques' penis hit a muscle in my bladder which then went into a spasm.

It was a muscle spasm! I was not dying; I was actually going to be ok.

I received a strong muscle relaxant and after a few minutes I was sent to the toilet to see if I was able to urinate. The pain finally subsided and my bladder's function returned to normal.

I was saved.

On the way back from the hospital, I was still very shaken by my ordeal. I kept asking myself what the hell had just happened and what I should do about it. It became very obvious to me that things could not keep going the way they were. Things needed to change. Sex things.

I needed information, help and education. We were still trying to get pregnant and I could not imagine risking any more visits to the emergency room.

I gave it some thought and remembered the word 'Tantra'. I had heard that word before in the media and knew that it had to do with some extraordinary sexual experiences. I really did not know where else to turn, so I decided to do some research. My analytical mind needed to understand what I was getting myself into.

That day marked the first day of the rest of my life. This is where my journey began. My story is still far from being finished but it has been absolutely extraordinary so far. I have learnt, experienced and witnessed things I never thought were possible before. I discovered a completely new way of being, of loving and living.

Since then I have never looked back and I feel extremely blessed to be on this path. It has been the most rewarding time of my life. After searching for something all my life and travelling the world for so many years, I found Tantra.

Finally, I was home.

Wounded healer

I once read an article with a very intriguing title along the lines of "Are you a shaman and do not know it". Of course I had to read it! Who does not want to know if they are a shaman?

The article listed a series of signs, characteristics and experiences that might potentially indicate that a person is indeed a shaman. I only remember one of the indicators as it spoke to me very strongly. According to the article, if you have experienced a significant crisis in some area of your life, it might have been your preparation, your 'initiation of fire' to heal and guide others in that area.

In a heartbeat I could identify one area of my life where I experienced not only a huge crisis but also frustration after frustration, pain, suffering, loneliness and hurt – sex. Also I did not personally know anybody else who had experiences similar to mine in their severity.

Many people do not talk to anybody about their sexual pain and disappointments. It is such a personal aspect of our lives. I definitely was not talking to anybody about it. I thought that there was some-thing wrong with me but I did not want to admit it to others. I felt ashamed and inadequate. I thought that I was the only person in the world who did not enjoy sex. After all, the media were full of naked people embraced in ecstasy. Sex in movies always ended in orgasm, and everybody seemed deeply aroused and satisfied by the experience.

When I started my sexual education – and later on my coaching practice – the truth soon became obvious to me. And the truth was that barely anybody that I was meeting was satisfied with their sex life! I welcomed the news with relief – I was not alone after all! But also with deep concern – what if most of our society was sexually frustrated and disillusioned? Where were the people who were having great sex? And what does it actually really mean to enjoy magical, intimate sexu-ality full of meaningful connection and orgasmic bliss?

I am fully aware that many people in the world suffer sexual abuse much worse than mine. I was never sexually abused as a child. I was never subject to a vicious sexual attack or suffered years of violent rape the way some people do in different parts of the globe. But in my own world, what I had been through was extreme enough to make me transform and bend, yet not so extreme that it would break my spirit.

I survived and my spirit survived. And now it was time to learn and heal.

PUTTING IT ALL TOGETHER

I would like to invite you to reflect upon your own relationship with sex, pleasure, touch and intimacy. Take a moment to think about your childhood and the messages that you were absorbing from your environment – your parents, siblings, extended family, friends, school, church, media …

Were you able to explore your sexuality as a child? What was your parents' approach to touch, self-touch and intimacy?

_____

_____

_____

_____

What is your first self-pleasuring memory and how did you feel about it?

_____

_____

_____

_____

What are your earliest sexual experiences?

_____

_____

_____

_____

What is the history of your masturbation?

_____

_____

_____

_____

What is the role of shame in your life?

_____

_____

_____

_____

What is your approach to self-touch right now?

_____

_____

_____

_____

Do you still touch yourself the same way you did ten years ago?

_____

_____

_____

_____

What is your self-pleasuring routine? Does it change much?

_____

_____

_____

_____

Do you use porn or fantasy? What kind?

_____

_____

_____

_____

What kind of people attract you the most?

_____

_____

_____

_____

Can you identify your core erotic theme?

_____

_____

_____

_____

Part 2

ENGAGING YOUR
BODY AND BREATH

"Breath is an inner lover, entering each cell of our bodies,
bringing pleasure and renewal to all parts of our being.
Breath is the mind's best teacher; breath helps the mind
open and release its anxieties. Breath is inspiration and
spirit. Breath happens unconsciously yet can be controlled
by our conscious minds; breath is a bridge. Breathing
fully, we engage the muscles of the pelvic floor and
stimulate the genital nerves. Breath is erotic and joyful."
— Caffyn Jesse, CSB.

EYE-GAZE WITH ME

After doing some online research on Tantra, I found evening work-shops being held in Melbourne. I checked with Jacques and then signed us both up for the upcoming event. I was extremely excited and could not wait to attend. Jacques did not share my enthusiasm but was happy to try something new.

After arriving at the venue, we met Stephanie from Tantric Synergy and a small group of other participants. Steph had a warm smile on her face and was very welcoming. We sat down and I kept my notepad and pen handy. I was not going to miss out on any profound teachings!

We learnt that Tantra was much more than sex; it was a way of being, of living your life where you experience everything fully, with full presence, awareness, with full intensity. Because by feeling more, we can enjoy more.

Stephanie explained that in our early lives, we learn to suppress and restrict our full expression and to live superficially. We learn to be good girls and boys who do not cry. We grow up to become pushovers and doormats, or bullies and machos. We learn to control our impulses so strongly that there is nothing wild and raw left in us. We become disconnected from our bodies and their needs. Tantra teaches us to connect again – to our bodies, to each other and to the Universe.

I felt the truth in Stephanie's words; they were resonating with me deeply. I heard an inner call to go back to nature, to live far away from civilization, to cultivate my connection to the Earth, plants and animals. I understood that the wonders of modern life might be actually a curse, turning us into a plastic society, addicted to media which keep feeding us lies or half-truths. I remembered hugging trees as a little girl, pulling carrots out of the ground in my grandparents' garden and eating them so fresh and juicy. No carrots from a supermarket ever tasted the same! I craved living in my body, connected and embodied, instead of living in my head, always near a computer screen.

Next, Stephanie explained the idea behind polarity. We all carry within us both masculine and feminine energy – our Shiva and Shakti. These polarities have nothing to do with gender; they represent two opposite forces that complete and balance each other, and they need each other to exist. The masculine energy of presence is a container for the feminine energy of movement and love. One force simply cannot express itself without the other; Shakti cannot dance without her Shiva holding space for her. This applies in sexuality – the masculine energy provides a solid, stable ground for the always moving feminine energy. Shiva is the consciousness while Shakti is dancing, giving birth to all creation.

This part confused me a little. I was not quite certain how to apply this Shiva-Shakti polarity in my relationship or how this was meant to help. But I was open to anything, like a sponge absorbing this new, exotic wisdom. And the romantic language of Tantra was speaking to my heart, my soul and my imagination.

Stephanie went on to explain that Tantra helps couples deal with the dilemma of men peaking much faster than women do, while at the same time offering both much deeper and more meaningful experiences. If I only knew that Steph was about to reveal the key to my struggles, my ears would have definitely perked up. But I was still clueless at that stage that all my lovers were in fact peaking way too fast, giving me no way to achieve a significant level of arousal.

Men in Tantra are taught to delay ejaculation and to actually separate it from the experience of orgasm. This way they can orgasm not only for much longer but also with their entire body, not just with the genitals. This allows for a much more satisfying experience. It takes a few months of training the body using breathing techniques and strengthening the pelvic floor muscle in order to achieve this skill. A conscious use of breath combined with tantric techniques allow the man to start moving his sexual energy up his spine and throughout his entire body, spreading the orgasmic feelings to his core, heart, throat and head.

I could see that Jacques was not convinced about the value of the non-ejaculatory practices. After all, we were still trying to get pregnant so it made no sense to ask him to withhold his semen. But I knew that anything we could learn here would be helpful and I was deeply craving anything pleasurable, satisfying or nurturing in bed.

Next Stephanie guided us through a beautiful eye-gazing practice. She explained that the couple should practice the breathing techniques together while softly gazing into each other's eyes. This brings a level of closeness and intimacy that many of us have never experienced before. At the same time it teaches us to remain present in the moment and aware of the other person – of what they are feeling and experiencing.

As I relaxed into the eye-gazing practice, I experienced a beautiful heart-opening in my chest, and feelings of joy and gratitude. At the same time I remained aware of Jacques' uneasiness and I worried that he would not enjoy it. But he shared with me that the whole world seemed to have disappeared as we were eye-gazing and that all he could see was me. I smiled. Maybe I was wrong. Maybe Jacques was enjoying these tantric teachings as much as I was. I was hopeful things were going to change.

Steph ended the workshop by telling us about the multitude of different kinds of orgasms that our bodies were capable of experiencing. She pointed to the wall behind us, which was filled with hundreds of books neatly resting on the floor to ceiling shelves. She said that if all these books talked about orgasms, they still would not exhaust the subject. We could even experience energetic orgasms without any touch required. You experience it by building up sexual energy in your genitals and then bringing it up along your chakras.

All this talk about moving energy in my body sounded like magic to me, but Steph insisted that once you start working with energy, it becomes as real as the table in the middle of the room. I was determined to explore that energy; I wanted to learn to feel it and to circulate it through my body. As soon as we got home, I started my practice.

I kept squeezing my pelvic floor muscle daily while using breathing practices. I was hoping to see results pretty quickly but nothing seemed to change. I did not feel any different – sex remained exactly the same. So I started to doubt. How was squeezing my PC muscle and breathing deeply going to make me tantric?

I started researching books about moving sexual energy and I came across a Taoist master, Mantak Chia, and his book *Cultivating female sexual energy*. It was very informative, and from it I learnt a practice of Microcosmic Orbit. Over some fifty pages and using many long and complicated words, Mantak explained that you can use your mind and muscle work to move energy from your perineum up your spine to the top of your head and then down the front of your body. With new enthusiasm, I incorporated the Microcosmic Orbit into my morning meditation practice. But weeks went by and I still could not sense any movement of energy in my body. Why was it so hard? I was getting frustrated again.

Disembodiment

The wall I was coming up against is the same problem many people in our society experience as a part of their everyday reality – disembodiment. I was so disconnected from my body that it took me a long time to start feeling subtle sensations and energetic shifts. They were always there but I was not aware of them. I had no idea what to look for, and my body was so shut down that I simply did not feel any sensations that did not involve direct, skin-on-skin friction.

Any traumatic or painful experiences can have that kind of effect on our bodies, particularly when experienced on an ongoing basis. As a result, we will soon develop an estrangement from our bodies, resenting the discomfort they are causing us. We might even feel like our bodies are letting us down if they do not perform the way we want them to perform. If they cause us pain and suffering. If they do not respond the way we wished they did.

The media is very efficient in taking this disembodiment even further, bombarding us with images of perfect, photo-shopped bodies, proving to us just how flawed we are and how much we need that product, that experience or that treatment. The message we hear in advertising every day is "you are not good enough, not beautiful enough, not slim enough, not attractive enough, you smell and are not cool; but once you buy our product, you will be ok".

How many people do you know who love their bodies? Who can stand naked in front of a full-length mirror and smile at what they see? Who can caress every inch of their skin with delight, appreciation and joy?

Men go through an additional programming around their genitals. Penises are often called 'that dirty thing' or 'that ugly thing' and are shamed and rejected by prude wives, girlfriends or lovers. Men are asked to cover up their private bits instead of being cherished and celebrated in their masculine essence. This is a very damaging approach and leaves a very real mark on men's psyches.

This really breaks my heart as no body part deserves that sort of poor treatment. A phallus was traditionally celebrated and honoured in different cultures. In Japan to this day people parade gigantic phallic-shaped shrines during a yearly festival of the penis and fertility. I feel like it is a great reminder of the sacred and special nature of the masculine body and genitalia. The penis is a very powerful and potent tool. It can cause great joy and healing, and also great pain and hurt. The more we reject and condemn it, the more we are pushing it towards unhealthy behaviours. The more we embrace and honour its vital nature, the more we can reclaim it and use it for good and joy.

Exercise:

Look at your own body. What do you feel? What do you notice? Where do your eyes wander first? Is it your round belly? Arms that are not muscular enough? Double chin? Thighs that rub each other? Wide feet? Big nose? Hairy back? We all hate something about ourselves because we keep buying into the fake ideal created by the media. While the truth is that every body is perfect and beautiful. There is no one shape that we all need to aspire to. We are all as unique as snowflakes. We are not meant to look the same. And we definitely are not meant to look like TV models – undernourished and over-exercised.

Denial and disconnection

I do believe in staying fit and healthy. At thirty years old I was 5 foot 4, 57 kilos and reasonably fit. I was making an effort to eat healthy and to go to the gym, do yoga and go for walks a few days a week. I had a slim figure with curvy hips, beautiful breasts, pretty face and guess what – I did not like my body.

It is imperative to develop a good relationship with your body in order to reach your full sexual potential. How can you feel waves upon waves of ecstatic pleasure when you are in bed with a partner if in your everyday life you are in denial about the reality of your body? If you are choosing to exist from the neck up, without much connection to your physical body? So many people live entirely in their heads from the moment they wake up to the moment they fall back asleep. They get up and put the TV on to watch the news, then they drive to the office and spend countless hours looking at the computer screen, analysing data, making phone calls, discussing outcomes. Then they get back home and spend an evening on the couch, remote control in their hand.

This is not how humans were designed to live. The human body is the only machine that gets better the more it is used. Before the civilized world created a system that effortlessly takes care of all our needs, we used to move much more – men would spend their days hunting for prey, women went gathering fruit or cultivating vegetables. We used to all gather at the end of the day to dance and connect with other members of our tribe. We used to be embodied, connected with ourselves, with others and with nature. Now we live in boxes, stare at boxes and become progressively more disconnected, frustrated and lonely.

Even worse, many people in our society develop what A.H. Almaas refers to as a 'genital hole'. It is a phenomenon where one's sexuality is so strongly repressed that the experience of any sensations in the genitals is extremely limited. That area of the body is literally experienced as a black hole. It is common in such cases to experience numbness, discomfort or pain when touched or stimulated sexually. Unfortunately, it is an everyday reality for many people who have suffered sexual abuse or negative sexual conditioning early on in their lives.

BUMPS ON THE ROAD

I was very excited to discover that there was a tantric massage therapist living nearby. I contacted him and he was happy to come to my place to run a session with me. Judging from his website, he seemed professional and experienced enough. I probably should have sought recommendations but I was determined – or rather desperate enough – to try anything.

While speaking on the phone, I described to him in short my issues with sexuality and the pain I was experiencing. He asked for my age and then stated that my case was urgent enough for him to come over the very next day. Once again I was too naïve to understand the real drive behind his keen interest in working with me.

Andrew was in his fifties, had a strong accent and was very nice. He used essential oils and a relaxing massage to put me in the mood. He massaged my entire body while I was lying on my front. He did not teach me any breathing techniques or give me any guidance or advice about what would happen during our time together. The relaxing part felt nice, but in no way prepared me for the rest of the session.

About half way in, he suddenly stuck his fingers inside my vagina and anus, without any warning or preparation. I jumped in pain on the table and he started to soothe me while keeping his fingers inside me. I was in torture and was wishing that he would stop. When he finally did, my whole body was shaking and I was wondering how much more of this 'healing' I was capable of taking.

He told me about other women he had worked with and how wet they got on his massage table, and about the amazing orgasms they experienced from his touch. I felt broken and envious. I wanted those results as well! So badly!

He told me that I should see him once a week and that slowly I would get better. I did in fact have two more sessions with him. Unfortunately, I completely suspended my own judgement and the wisdom of my body. I put my entire trust in him, disregarding all the signals that my system was sending me – the pain, the discomfort and the tension Andrew was causing within me.

All three sessions were fairly similar; however, he did become a little gentler with my genitals in sessions two and three. Back then I did not know that people were able to take through their touch instead of giving. I was absolutely certain that Andrew was touching me for my benefit only. After all, he was getting paid for it. However, in the light of my current experience and knowledge, I cannot help but wonder whether his intentions were indeed as pure as I assumed at the time. It is my strong suspicion that he might have been much more concerned about his own pleasure than mine.

In our third and last session together, at some point he laid down next to me and insisted that I licked his fingers while he was massaging my body with the other hand. I simply could not do it, and decided that sessions with him were too much for me to bear. Surely there were easier ways to get better! I just needed to find a better practitioner to work with. A female practitioner.

I was sufficiently put off working with men that it took me over a year before I would allow another man in a professional capacity to touch my body.

De-armouring

It is way too easy to re-traumatize a client if the practitioner is not careful or experienced enough. Through my own tantric education and practice, I learned first-hand about the value of presence and loving compassion when working with people who have suffered abuse. When looking back at the sessions with Andrew, I still wonder whether he was consciously and cruelly taking advantage of me, or whether he was genuinely trying to help me but my case overwhelmed him and he did not know how to best handle me.

I do not carry anger or resentment towards him, but simply value the experience he gave me. It was important for me to know what exactly happens in the tantric industry so that I could potentially warn others who rely on my professional expertise. In fact, I would never recommend a practitioner that I did not receive a session from myself – and obviously only if I was happy with that session.

What is important for men in our society to know is that the majority of women have had some version of this experience. Whether from a partner, a friend, a co-worker, a body-worker or a stranger, many women have been touched in a way that was not invited, not appropriate or not pleasant. And it is our body's natural mechanism to protect itself from unwanted touch by creating tension and numbness. This is what the process of armouring refers to.

Imagine the hands of a construction worker. As he handles rough surfaces month after month, he eventually develops hard skin and calluses on his palms. Our genitals become hardened not so much physically but energetically. A certain level of tension will be held in a woman's genitals over time, which will lead to lessened sensations. This is her body's protection mechanism. This mechanism protects her from pain, but also from pleasure.

When you encounter a girl who asks for hard and fast sex, it is either because she believes that this is what the guy wants (and she wants to please the guy) or because she is so desensitized that this is the only way for her to feel anything.

The good news is that body armouring is reversible and every man is capable of helping his woman heal. Every man carries in his trousers a very potent tool, capable of both healing and wounding. A conscious penis used with the right intention can draw years of trauma and hurt out of a vagina. How to do it? I'm glad that you asked!

Exercise:

Next time you are intimate with your partner, treat her genitals like you would a small, wounded child. Slow down, be gentle, do not push or force anything to happen. Treat her body with love, compassion and respect. When you penetrate her, remain absolutely present with her, do not lose yourself in your own pleasure. Give her your entire attention. Allow this time to be all about her.

Start by resting the head of your penis at the entrance of her vagina. There is no rush, just stay there. Notice what you are feeling in your body. Ask her what she is feeling. Invite her to become aware of and maybe even verbalize any sensations, emotions or realizations that she might be having. Give her time; do not pressure her to move on.

Whenever she is ready – and using lubrication if necessary – move a centimetre in and then stay completely still again. Encourage her to keep breathing and to relax. Many people automatically tense up and shorten their breath in a sexual situation. But the more relaxed she is, the more beneficial this process will be for her. Reassure her that you are enjoying this and that she can take all the time she needs. Tell her that this is your gift to her.

Keep moving in centimetre by centimetre, and then stay still and allow her to keep building awareness and sensation in her vaginal canal. Feel free to spend half an hour doing this process – or even an hour if you are generous enough and if you are both willing. Give extra time to any areas where she feels more discomfort. Encourage her to notice any areas where she feels pleasure. Help her re-sensitize any spots that feel numb and eventually reclaim her entire vagina as an erotic, pleasurable part of her body. You might need to repeat this process a few times, depending on her level of armouring.

Remember not to take from her – this is not about your pleasure, but about hers. It is absolutely fine if you sincerely enjoy this process, but do not be guided in it by your own pleasure. Maintain the intention of service throughout the experience.

YOUNG LOVERS

After three and a half years together, my relationship with Jacques finally ended. We simply grew apart so much that we barely shared anything anymore, apart from a house and an occasional meal. I was studying Tantra and spiritual arts while he did not even want to hear about exploring these realms with me anymore. I was morphing into a new person while he remained where he was before. Common ground was getting thinner and thinner.

When I moved out, I continued my tantric practice all by myself. But fortunately I did not have to wait long for a new lover.

While I was still with Jacques, I explored different options to heal my daddy-issues – spiritual hypnotherapy, kinesiology and a shamanic tool called aspecting. I was slowly healing my need to make older men love me. When you shine a light of awareness on to any dark, wounded aspects of yourself, that darkness can become conscious and can start to dissipate. Through presence comes understanding and through that comes a resolution.

Stanley was only five years older than me and I found him very handsome, funny and smart. He was interested in me from the very first time that we met, and I was loving his attention. In many ways he was a polar opposite of Jacques and that was soothing to me after all the pain I went through during the breakup.

Jacques was strong and dominant, a typical alpha male. He always wanted things his way and he knew exactly what he wanted. He was born to rule and conquer. Stanley was very concerned about my opinion and wanted to please me very much. Nothing I wanted was a problem for him and he felt like the luckiest man alive to have me.

In bed he was very caring and generous. He could last a long time and actually wanted me to orgasm as well. At that stage vaginal orgasms were still a mystery to me, but I was keen to play and explore sex with my new man.

My tantric library kept growing as I was buying and reading anything related to Tantra that I could find. Diana Richardson was one of my first teachers, and her books were consistently advising me that relaxation in sex was absolutely necessary for orgasms. And so I kept relaxing as hard as I could but those orgasmic peaks kept eluding me. Night after night I was witnessing Stanley's ecstatic pleasure while I was crying inside, wondering why I could not join him there.

I knew that breath was another key aspect of this equation in which you add all the pieces together and an orgasm results at the end. Deep conscious belly breath. I was making sure that I was not holding my breath but that it was flowing in a full, rhythmic way.

I played with a vibrator sometimes in an attempt to climax during sex. While I was sitting on top of my lover, I would hold the vibrating toy against my clitoris but it was not proving successful. I needed my entire attention to be placed on my clit long enough for that clitoral orgasm to happen, and Stanley's penis thrusting in and out was distracting me too much. I felt doomed.

But amidst much impatience and disappointment, I was experiencing little wins here and there. Slowly, slowly my body was opening and all the tantric knowledge I was soaking up was starting to make a difference.

On top of relaxation and breath I started to add another element – presence. Instead of staying in my head, thinking, worrying or analysing the experience, I started to place my attention inside of my body. I still remember the first time I did this. Stanley was lovingly penetrating my vagina and so I focused all my attention there. I was absolutely shocked to realize that my pleasure and sensations were at least tripled from this little practice alone.

One of the big reasons for disembodiment is that we are thinking instead of feeling. And that was definitely my case. I was slowly learning to let go of the mind and to completely immerse myself in the experience of sex, in my bodily sensations. Instead of thinking about the experience of sex, I was finally *having* the experience of sex.

Body epiphany

What I was going through is described as 'body epiphany' by Ed Maupin[4]. This is a personal experience in which the reality of the body becomes very clear to the individual. We start to realize just how strongly mind and body are connected and that we are not just heads on sticks. Little by little, we fully discover that we have bodies full of wisdom and that these bodies are constantly communicating with us.

We learn to perceive reality differently; we take it in through not only our minds but through our bodies as well. We start to pay close attention to the clues the body is giving us. We start to notice just how differently the body feels when we are overwhelmed with pressure at work, when we are held in an embrace by a loved one, when we eat too much or just after a workout.

We pay more attention to our five senses and we take the world in more mindfully. Through a stronger sensory awareness, we are able to enjoy our experiences more and to show up more in our lives – for ourselves and for others.

Embodiment is absolutely crucial for deepening our erotic experience. If you look again at your most memorable sexual experiences, you will most certainly notice that they happened while you were completely and intensely present in the experience. You were right there, completely there, without a thought about the world around you.

Exercise:

I would like to invite you to a little self-enquiry. Close your eyes, take a few deep breaths and start noticing all the different sensations in your body. Take your time and observe everything that you are feeling. When I first tried this exercise, I could not come up with one thing I was feeling. When I do it now, I notice the pressure of the chair on my legs and buttocks, the floor under my feet. I can feel mild tension behind my right eyebrow. I notice the air flowing through my nostrils. I delight in gentle tingles flowing down my arms as I allow my hands to relax in my lap. I feel a gentle tickle on my chin. A wave of relaxation in my shoulders. My heartbeat. A relaxed rhythm of my chest raising and falling with each breath. Etc., etc., etc.

Body scan

I am going to share with you a process that, when performed regularly, will start to re-sensitize you and bring more awareness and more sensation into your body. The body scan has been performed by people all over the world for millennia and is a simple meditation practice.

Exercise:

Start by settling into a comfortable position with the palms of your hands facing up. Take a few deep breaths. Let go of any distractions and just stay with your breath for a few moments, noticing each inhale and each exhale. Next, place your awareness in your fingers and start noticing what they feel like. What are you sensing? What does it feel like to have fingers? Are you noticing any energy there? Vibration? Tingles? Aliveness? Or nothing at all? Stay for a few moments with whatever arises. And then expand your awareness to the palms of your hands and repeat the process. So now you are placing your attention on both your fingers and the palms of your hands. Whenever you are ready, keep expanding your awareness into your wrists, arms, elbows, shoulders. Next, move on to your toes, soles of your feet, your heels, calves, knees, thighs, genitals, hips, belly, lower back, chest, upper back, neck, back of your neck, your face, back of your head and finally the top of your head. After you have spent a few moments with each part of your body, simply give yourself a few more moments to enjoy the sensations in your entire body. Notice the sense of aliveness permeating your entire being.

Pleasure in awareness

Can you see just how much sensation there is in your body already? We just need to become more connected, more present in our bodies.

Quite frankly, it blows my mind just how much pleasure I can feel in my body when my attention is entirely focused within. The moment I become distracted and my mind wanders, the sensations drop by as much as 90%! And yet we all allow our attention to wander. Some people are so disembodied that they are capable of missing an orgasm! According to the Medical Daily website (www.medicaldaily. com): "Women can have orgasms and not always be aware of it. Typical orgasm indicators such as specific breathing patterns, body movements, vocalizations, and muscle contractions may not always be present."[5] Can you imagine being in a state of orgasm without realizing it?

Start using the body scan today. Use it daily or as often as you can. It does not have to take a long time; anything between three and twenty minutes will work. Obviously, the more committed you are to this practice, the better the results you will achieve.

And definitely try this before sex! You will thank me later!

BREATHE YOUR BODY ORGASMIC

Around that time I got a hold of a book by Barbara Carrellas titled *Urban Tantra*[6]. Barbara is a very inspiring sex educator and has many years of experience in the field of Tantra. She is based in New York City and has done amazing work to create a system of tantric practices for people who are unable to escape the city landscape in order to practice in nature. She also speaks very strongly for gender fluidity issues and is very creative at embracing kink and BDSM practices in her work.

She strongly recommends using breath to access profound ecstatic states. The book lists many different breathing techniques, but two of them in particular played a role in my sexual awakening.

Barbara describes a practice of focusing your awareness and 'breathing into' a body part in order to re-sensitize it[7]. The book invites you to imagine that one of your fingers is a lung and that you are drawing air into it as you inhale. As you keep breathing in and out of your finger, placing your whole attention in it, you will quickly discover that this particular finger feels very different to all the other ones. It becomes full of life, full of awareness, almost buzzing with different sensations.

So I tried it one day but instead of a finger, I used my genitals. Three times within a space of one day I took a few minutes to breathe into my vagina. It felt nice to connect to her. As I kept breathing, I allowed her to relax, to open; I was imagining that my breath was travelling past my lungs, past my belly, all the way down to her.

That same evening I saw Stanley and things got intimate. Soon he was inside me as we held each other in a loving embrace. And as we kept going, I noticed something strange happening inside me. I could not help but ask him, completely puzzled, "Have you ejaculated?". He denied it and I knew that he had not, but the amount of liquid within my vaginal canal was a completely new experience to me. I was lubricating like crazy and it felt amazing! I must honestly say that I had never been this wet in my entire life.

I commented on it and Stanley agreed. He was proud of himself for my level of arousal but I knew that it was not him, it was Barbara. Well, the breathing technique that she taught me.

I use this technique to this day whenever I am driving, reading, relaxing … In particular if I am getting ready to see a lover. Or if I am about to self-pleasure. It feels so good to breathe into my genitals that sometimes I do not need to touch myself at all as my breath is slowly, gently bringing more and more arousal, pleasure and sensation into my body. Think of your breath as a lover, caressing you with softness and sensuality.

Another one of Barbara's breathing techniques that I enjoyed exploring was a Firebreath[8] involving the system of chakras and aimed at taking you into a full-body orgasm. I had heard about full-body, energetic orgasms for a while now and I was keen to experience them for myself. The chakra system comes from Eastern traditions and describes seven energy centres spread from the base of the spine to the top of the head. If you are not familiar with the chakra system, look it up online and you will find a lot of images and references.

I decided to play with the Firebreath as I went to bed in the evening. I laid down, relaxed my body and took a few deep breaths. I began by focusing on my base chakra (located at the bottom of the spine) and started inhaling and drawing energy from the Earth into it. I was visualizing it as a wheel of red colour spinning inside of my body. With each inhale the red wheel was getting stronger, bigger and more intense. Next, I moved on to my second chakra located above my genitals. I kept drawing energy up from the base chakra and visualizing the second chakra as a spinning wheel of orange colour. When my sacral chakra felt strong and intense enough, I moved up again to my solar plexus. I kept going through my heart, throat, third eye and finally into my crown chakra. Each time I was bringing energy up into the chakra, energizing it and saturating it with colour and intensity.

When I finally made my way up to the top of my head, I suddenly had to stop the exercise as my whole being dissolved into an amazing state of absolute bliss. I still have no words to describe how it felt. I did not even know that it was possible to feel this way! It was like a state of deep trance where my mind was completely free of thought and every cell of my body was gently vibrating with pleasure. I was not doing anything anymore, I was just being. I did not want this experience to end but eventually I fell asleep.

Yes, I was definitely sold on the concept of using breath in my erotic practice. I kept playing and experimenting with different breathing techniques, including the ones designed to take you into a full-body orgasm. At that stage my results were varied and inconsistent, which was frustrating me. But at the same time I knew that I was finally getting somewhere. And that my breath was a crucial component of the puzzle.

Belly breathing

In our modern society we do not give breath the respect that it deserves. We usually take it for granted and we do not think much about it. Our brain is designed so well that it automatically takes care of the function of the breath without the need for our conscious control.

However, breath is very special in that – unlike other automatic functions of the body – you can actually use your awareness to control it. You cannot easily control your heart rate or your digestion process. But you definitely can control your breath!

Our society is full of chest breathers. It is quite uncommon to see someone breathing deeply into their belly. We all tend to keep our breath shallow and short. Unfortunately, this limits significantly the amount of energy you have and the amount of sensations you can feel in your body. I like to challenge my clients to spend an entire day breathing deeply, fully. They usually report back to me quite surprised at how much more alive and energetic their body feels as a result.

In fact, chest breathing is not a natural behaviour. When you observe little children, you will notice that they breathe into their bellies. As a result, they are all ecstatic – they are running around, laughing, positive energy exploding throughout their happy bodies.

And then one day we tell them off. They are told, often with irritation, to sit still, to stop making noise and being naughty. So children learn early that this vibrant aliveness in their bodies can get them into trouble and they start to constrict their breath, slowly becoming adults who only take short, shallow breaths.

When we breathe deeply, the air can travel deep into our bodies, oxygenating all our cells and expanding our sensory awareness. But when we only take short, shallow breaths, the results will be limited.

Remember, the more you breathe, the more you feel!

Exercise:

Spend one day taking full, deep, conscious breaths. Set up reminders on your phone as you'll likely forget about your breath while being busy with work and other activities.

At the end of the day reflect – how did you experience your body today? Did it feel different? More alive? More vibrant?

If possible, make love that evening – to your partner or to yourself. Keep the breath full and relaxed. Keep noticing the intensity of sensations in your body.

FULL-BODY ORGASMS

After having a few experiences of hit and miss with tantric practitioners, I went back to see Stephanie from Tantric Synergy. I guess I wanted to learn from a variety of people instead of having one 'guru', but I definitely do wish that I had decided to see Steph sooner. I told her about my journey so far and asked if she could help me become more orgasmic. She was happy to help and we scheduled a session.

When I arrived, we started with a chat. I described my experiences and efforts and she offered her insights. But everything that she was telling me I had already read or heard before. I already knew all about relaxing, surrendering, staying present and using my breath. I knew about the male/female polarity and how it played out in sex. All the theory and information was in my head, I just could not get my body to experience it.

Stephanie proposed that we do a yoni massage. Yoni (pronounced as yo-nee) is a Sanskrit word for female genitalia and means 'sacred space'. I agreed and was handed a sarong. I undressed, wrapped the sarong around my body and we began. Steph took me through a beautiful ritual where words like 'cosmos', 'sisters journeying together' and 'energy' came up. I allowed myself to enjoy the mystical ambience she was creating.

Steph remained very gentle and respectful as I lay down and removed my sarong. It was a completely different experience to the massage provided by Andrew a few months before. Now my body was being treated like a temple, honoured by conscious touch and a loving presence.

Stephanie sat between my legs and began the massage. I was menstruating so she limited the touch to external strokes. As she was gently caressing my vulva, my sexual energy began to build up and flow. Her touch felt so amazing, so soft, so pleasurable!

She directed me to use breath, sound and movement during the session, so soon we began to spread and circulate that erotic charge through my entire body. Before long my whole body was tingling with intense pleasure and bliss. It felt so good; I could have stayed there forever!

This experience was a big a-ha! moment for me. This whole talk about full-body orgasms, energetic orgasms, chakra orgasms, etc., still kept me wondering about the role of the genital response during these experiences. Just like many people in our society, I was used to thinking of orgasm as a series of pleasurable pulsating sensations in the pelvic floor region. So I kept wondering – do full-body orgasms come with these muscle spasms as well? And how does it happen if in many cases the genitals are not stimulated at all – as in during breathing orgasms?

Now I finally knew.

Stephanie guided my body to a full-body orgasmic state and kept me there for a while. But even though she did stroke my genitals, I did not experience the familiar pulsating response that I was used to before. Instead my entire body seemed to be pulsating blissfully during – and for many hours after – the session.

Moving sexual energy

Since that time I have facilitated and witnessed hundreds of similar experiences for my clients. In fact, I almost daily guide clients to a full-body sexual awakening, and the responses are usually nothing short of amazement. Both men and women respond to tantric techniques equally, allowing these tools and practices to take them gently and gracefully into a deeper embodiment, profound sensuality and mind-blowing pleasure.

The experience of awakening and channelling up one's sexual energy is in some traditions referred to as Kundalini awakening. Kundalini energy is our life force energy, aka our sexual energy. It is portrayed as a snake coiled three and a half times around the base of the spine. As you awaken the snake, it stretches up your spine to the top of your head, allowing a wonderful internal release of this strong energy through the entire system.

Many people do not realize just how potent their sexual energy is. In our sexually repressed society, we learn to keep our erotic charge only in our genitals until we are ready to release it out of the body in an ejaculatory orgasm for men, or a clitoral orgasm for women. Conventionally, as we get aroused, we tense up our bodies and constrict or even hold our breath. Both these responses lock arousal in our genitals and do not allow it to travel through the body. This scenario gives us a very localized, genitally based, release-type of experience. And as much as it can feel very nice, there is much more out there for us to explore.

This is why in Tantra we relax our bodies. It is not about being limp; you can absolutely stay active and relaxed. It is simply about not holding tension in your body which would inhibit your ecstatic experience. And this is also why we breathe deeply, freely. Your breath will literally carry your sexual energy all throughout your body. If you allow it.

Just think – your sexual energy is capable of producing a new life, a child! Isn't that just magnificent? And what happens when you start to move and circulate that potent life force inside of your own body? You are creating more life for yourself.

Tantrics believe that sexual energy is capable of healing us, energizing us, rejuvenating our bodies, clearing our minds and inspiring our thinking. Tantric men who circulate their sexual energy regularly report that they do not need as much sleep. They feel much more energized during the day. They do not get sick as much. And they experience an amazing clarity of thinking and a profound creativity.

Men often tell me about a certain fogginess they experience in their brains after ejaculating. On top of that, it is no secret that after the release the man is most likely going to roll over and fall asleep as his body is feeling drained and depleted. These and other symptoms can be largely reduced if sexual energy is spread through the entire body first and maybe even kept within the body as the man develops an ability to experience non-ejaculatory orgasms.

The truth is that all men can be multi-orgasmic. All men can experience full-body, deeply nurturing, energizing and satisfying ecstatic states. But in order to get there, they first need to learn to separate ejaculation from orgasm.

Addictive release

I used to think that men were the lucky ones in sex. After all they could orgasm pretty much every single time, which is something I had struggled with for so many years. Now I am aware that this ease of ejaculating can actually be a much more serious problem.

These release-type experiences can definitely provide men with a few seconds of intense pleasure but, in the end, they always result in depletion as a large amount of energy is lost in the process. As the man becomes drained of his life force every single time, the satisfaction he derives from each ejaculation is very short-lived and soon he needs to masturbate or have sex again. This can lead to a vicious cycle and an addiction to the release. Always chasing it but never achieving enough satisfaction from it.

Women's sexuality is not so strongly centred on the release. In fact, many women do not orgasm during sex at all so they enjoy the experience for the sheer pleasure it gives them. This allows the woman to sensually savour the nice feelings in her body without getting too fixated on her genital response.

For this reason many women are naturally tantric, and it is much easier for them to master full-body orgasms than it is for men.

Please remember, as long as you are chasing that ejaculatory response, you will not be able to reach your full orgasmic potential or provide a deeply ecstatic experience to your partner. Women, on average, take four times as long as men do to orgasm. This means that the longer you can last, the longer you can just stay in arousal without trying to get anywhere, the more likely she will be to reach a level of arousal high enough to take her over the edge of a massive orgasm.

THE REAL TANTRA

My relentless pursuit of tantric knowledge and experience kept taking me to different workshops, trainings and events run all over the world. I studied with teachers from all corners of Australia, from New Zealand, the USA and Europe. I was fascinated by the variety of approaches and different methods presented and used. Everybody seemed to have their own version of Tantra and their own way to practice it. It did not bother me in the slightest; I figured everybody had a piece of the puzzle and from these different teachings and elements, the real Tantra would emerge.

When I first heard about the International School of Temple Arts, I was not convinced that I needed to attend their training. Their week-long Spiritual Sexual Shamanic Experience did not seem to make any tantric promises to me. However, testimonials and recommendations were pretty uniform – do it!

I finally made up my mind about two weeks before the event started. But when I headed to the website to commit myself, I learned that the event was being held at a venue in the middle of a forest where we all were going to bunk together in dorms.

In dorms!

I was immediately taken aback. I did not want to sleep in dorms with strangers! Is it not what young people do when they cannot afford a hotel? Are you not meant to upgrade to a better quality accommodation once you have a job?

I was used to hotels and to having my own bathroom. This dorm experience was going to test me for sure.

My heart filled with anxiety, I settled the fee and scheduled the event in my calendar.

And so two weeks later I flew to New Zealand and met up with other participants. We made our way into the bush and stayed there for a whole week without access to the internet, phone service, shops, bars or anybody else. Just a group of thirty people, Mother Nature and glow worms. And big spiders in the bathroom.

That week in the forest was one of the most intense experiences of my life! The dorms were no problem at all and actually brought us all very close together. We became a tribe, a family. We laughed together, we ate together, we learned together. As the week went on, we cried, we screamed and we healed together. We held each other with deep compassion as we were learning to hold ourselves, to become deeply embodied, authentically raw and true to ourselves.

I learned that apart from the brain in my head, I also have two other brains – one in my heart and one in my belly. And that I should listen to all of them, not only to the one in my head.

We all know the brain between our ears – it is busy with thoughts, with intellect. It analyses data and seeks solutions. It helps us memorize information and make logical decisions. But this is just one way to 'think'.

We also have a brain in our gut which is more commonly known as the 'gut feeling'. We actually have a fairly complex neural network contained within our digestive system that has a huge impact on the way we feel, and on our emotional state. Your gut brain is called the Enteric Nervous System and it communicates with you through different sensations – intuition, butterflies in your tummy, that bad feeling about someone that you cannot explain, the feeling that you just know but do not know how, or that painful tension in your belly when you are feeling rejected.

And finally – but most importantly – your heart brain, your emotional centre. Your emotions constitute a very sophisticated feedback system that is there to support your decision-making process. Remember the time when you acted out of passion even though your decision made no logical sense? Or when you really, really wanted to do something even though it was not – intellectually – the smartest choice? It was your heart talking to you.

During the training we were told that in order to be fully authentic, you need to receive a 'yes' or a 'no' from all three brains in your body. That a 'yes' from the head, unsupported by the gut or the heart is not a fully authentic 'yes'. I have since read an opinion that as long as you listen to your heart brain, everything will always work out for you. I do not think that this is entirely true, but I definitely do love the sentiment behind it. I am actually leaning toward the opinion presented by The School of Life in their video: *Why You Shouldn't Trust Your Feelings*: "For a range of historical reasons, we've collectively been extremely reluctant to recognize the benefits of emotional skepticism. (...) We would have gone a long way to counteract the problems of our minds if we sometimes do ourselves the honour of not listening to our feelings, instead waiting for certain unhelpful moods to pass and accepting that we are at heart highly viscous bags of saline solution who stare out at reality via a highly unreliable and distorted pane of glass and must therefore frequently suspend judgement, moderate our impulses, watch over our diet and strive to get to bed early."[9]

When in an emotional storm, I always recommend taking a break, having a tea, counting to ten, going for a walk or doing anything else that allows you to calm down and reconnect with your authentic self. Only in this way you can authentically figure out what it is that you want or do not want.

And so for the first time in my life I started to own my 'yes' and my 'no'. The truth is that I never actually knew how to say 'no' before. I was always so worried about not being liked that I would always say 'yes' and then I would do my best to wiggle myself out of a situation, hoping that it would go away. Or if it did not, I would resentfully do what I was asked to do. Women in general are strongly conditioned to seek the approval of others, while men usually are not so bothered about it and so it is much easier for them to say 'no'.

I was pretty shaken to the core, but also extremely proud of myself when I actually heard myself say 'no' to someone at the venue. I did it respectfully and politely. Nevertheless I did it, and it was authentic.

Authenticity

We all put masks on for others. We do our best to seem smarter, funnier, more attractive, etc. But deep down we all crave someone authentic and true. When we notice that someone is trying too hard for us, when they are making too much of an effort to please us, we start to lose interest.

How authentic are you in your relating to other people? How is your 'yes' and your 'no'? Do they come only from the head? What do you base your decisions on? What do you feel when you make them?

Exercise:

Next time you are faced with a choice, I invite you to consider all three of your brains before giving an answer. Do not only go with the logical outcome. Consider your gut feeling about it. Listen to your heart. Really feel into the choice you are making. How does each option make you feel? Find the one which brings the most alignment between your three thinking centres.

Make sure that from now on you do not only think but also feel your way through life.

YONI MAPPING

So I figured it was time to go see Stephanie from Tantric Synergy again. I still had a lot of healing to do and I was not going to stop. This time we decided to do yoni mapping. In a way, this is a similar process to the healing technique that I described in Part 1; however, instead of using the penis, the practitioner uses fingers.

Once again Steph welcomed me with warmth, love and compassion. She helped me relax on my back before she started the process of mapping.

Genital mapping simply means holding with awareness different points on the genital structure while the person being worked on connects, relaxes and breathes into each point. The practitioner can hold any number of points in different locations, but in the case of female genitalia, it is a common practice to work around the vaginal canal, holding four to twelve points internally. If time permits, it can be useful to repeat this process at different depths, depending on the agreement made beforehand.

Steph held about eight points, working her way around my vagina, starting at my G-spot. At each point she guided me to use my breath and to really feel into the area she was holding. She was asking me to express what I was feeling. I was meant to look for pleasure, pain, numbness, discomfort or any emotions.

My vagina had experienced a lot of trauma through years of mechanical thrusting by insensitive or unaware lovers. When I look back at all different men that I ever slept with before finding the path of Tantra, I recall often feeling like a masturbation device. With lights off and eyes tightly shut, these men were completely lost in their own pleasure, chasing that point of release. They did not even seem interested in what I was feeling, although I am certain that they would have loved to hear that they gave me an amazing experience.

I never blamed them for the discomfort and frustration I was experiencing. They did not know any better, nor did I. We were all completely clueless and disconnected, oblivious to the world of sexual delights that was possible once one decided to seek some proper education.

So my vagina kept armouring herself more and more while my cervix was completely numb after being exposed to years of mindless pounding. All men love deep penetration. But for a woman with a short vaginal canal that means trouble. I was always able to touch my own cervix with a finger, which should give you an idea of how close it is to my vaginal opening.

The cervix is actually an amazing body part that can easily lift out of the way when a woman is aroused. But I rarely was. And so sex was painful.

The session with Steph was a big step on my healing journey. As we kept moving from one point to the next, I was discovering with shock and sadness that there was not one spot in my vagina that felt pleasurable.

All I was experiencing was discomfort, pain or numbness. Some of the points were also holding emotional trauma locked in a chronic tension. Under Steph's caring touch, the tension started to dissipate, freeing old emotions of sadness, anger, grief and frustration. About half way through the process I started to cry and scream in despair. The waves of emotions being released through my body were overwhelmingly strong. But I was finally processing them out of my body; I was letting them go.

When I got home after the session, broken-hearted and grieving, all I wanted to do was to be alone and cry. All I could do was nurture myself and sleep.

I was not healed yet. But I was getting better.

Sexual communication

If you suspect that your partner might be holding tension in her vagina, and particularly if she feels numb or uncomfortable during sex, you should recommend that she see a Tantra practitioner for a genital mapping session. You can also assist her yourself as this practice is fairly simple. What it does require is time, patience, love, compassion and a whole lot of mindfulness!

As you are holding a series of points inside her vagina, make sure to keep paying very close attention to the responses of her body. Look at her face, notice her breathing pattern, look for signs of tension in her body. It is also very important to maintain an excellent communication throughout the experience. Many people feel uncomfortable with talking about their sexuality. Often we have no idea how to even find the words to communicate during sex, touch or any intimate activity.

Do you ever find yourself questioning whether she is enjoying your touch if she is just lying there without a sound? Would you like to have a simple system allowing you to find out just how much your partner is enjoying your caresses? A system that would help you find out what it is that she would really like? A simple feedback system which would allow you both to have the most perfect experience together?

I am going to let you in on a little secret – a system like that exists, and it is simpler to use than you think.

Many people make a mistake of asking "is this ok?'. Many things are ok without being overly good or overly bad, so this is a poorly worded question. As long as you are not hurting her, she will most likely say that yes, it is ok. But this is not what we are looking for. We are looking for exact information that will allow you to alter your touch so that she can have the most ideal experience with you.

Exercise:

Start by making it easy for her – give her choices. "Would you like this firmer or softer?" "Would you like this faster or slower?" "Deeper or shallower thrusts?" "Would you like me to use my tongue only or also my lips?" If you are still uncertain, ask her to show you. "Please take my hand and guide it to show me how you like to be touched here."

Stay attuned

Please bear in mind that her level of sensitivity will change as her arousal grows. But it is always safer to err on the side of caution and start by touching her too lightly rather than too firmly. A touch that is too firm too quickly will trigger her protection mechanism, and her body will tense up. And that is definitely not what you want.

If you are taking her through a yoni mapping process, it is crucial to communicate with her and to find the right kind of pressure appropriate for each point. This kind of work is very intuitive. If you really want to assist her with healing, you need to remain closely tuned in to her on the energetic level. Our bodies send many signals that are too subtle to be noticed consciously. So as she is feeling into different points held by you, you should also make sure to feel, observe and notice with your mind, your soul and your heart.

And finally, let go of any goals; each genital mapping session looks different. Do not expect your partner to achieve any particular outcome. Simply allow her to have her own experience.

YOGA-GASM

My orgasmic practice kept moving along nicely, and I actually started to experience new kinds of orgasm on a regular basis. The energetic orgasms became easier and easier to achieve and even though I was still not orgasming during sex, I had a rich orgasmic practice in my solo-explorations.

What was even more exciting was that orgasms started to surprise me in places and situations that I would not have considered orgasmic or even sexual before. I was learning what it meant to live an ecstatic life both in the bedroom and outside of it.

One morning, as usual, I unrolled my mat and began my day with a yoga practice. As I was moving through a series of asanas, I kept pondering the fact of energy flowing through our bodies. When this is happening with intensity, as in during a physical effort, we experience aliveness and vibrancy within ourselves. Unfortunately, this vibrancy can often go unnoticed if we do not pay enough attention to actually sense it, to feel what is happening. We hold too much tension, we are too much in the head or we are simply not used to noticing sensations in our bodies.

I had previously worked with a client whom I guided into a full-body orgasm during our session. As he entered the experience, he suddenly opened his eyes and looked at me, pulling himself out of the orgasm. I gently guided him back into his body, but it became apparent to me that he was not actually 'feeling' the waves of ecstatic flow in his body. Instead he was stuck in his head questioning what was meant to happen and whether he was 'doing it right'.

I relaxed into Savasana to complete my yoga practice and I joyously felt my body relaxing on the floor. It was simply divine to feel my energy flowing gently as my yoga practice was not too strenuous. So it definitely caught me by surprise when my body suddenly started to shake in ecstasy, shifting into a full-body orgasmic state. I kept breathing deeply to support the energetic flow, and remained very relaxed to allow the energy to do what it wanted to do.

It felt amazingly nurturing to start my day energized by my life force. We are so lucky to be able to access this deeply potent source of vitality, strength and bliss right here, inside of our bodies.

I do believe that it is our birthright to be orgasmic.

Your orgasmic potential

Once you commit yourself to the path of exploring your orgasmic potential, you come across many different types, intensities and structures of orgasm. At first you will most likely explore the gender-specific genital types – ejaculatory or anal orgasm for you and clitoral, G-spot, vaginal, cervical, anal orgasms for her. Your further tantric studies will no doubt take you to energetic and full-body orgasms. And you will think that you have conquered the world, but it is still just the beginning.

As you keep connecting deeper and deeper to your body, mind, heart and soul, you will start discovering the emotional body orgasms – cry-gasms, anger-gasms, laughter-gasms, etc. You will also discover that in fact your entire body is an erogenous zone and that you can experience orgasms in your chest, head, arms, fingers, belly, legs and so on – focused in that particular body part or in connection with the rest of the body.

And if you keep delving deeper into your soul and your spiritual side, you might discover that some orgasms feel like you are connecting with the whole Universe and that you are expanding well beyond the boundaries of your physical self.

Exercise:

The easiest way to start entering the orgasmic realm more often is to use movement. You can dance, shake, run, box or use any other exercise that will bring a lot of energy into your body. Give yourself ten minutes of physical effort, but really commit to it. Make sure that your heart rate increases and that you are breaking some sweat.

Once you are done, lie down on your back, relax and simply allow yourself to experience the energetic storm happening in your body. Allow the energy to move you and to move through you. Completely surrender to it. If you feel like your body wants to move in any way, allow it.

This is a very beautiful experience of surrender and of dissolving into bliss. It might take you a few tries to achieve a deep state of ecstatic pleasure. And if you are struggling, remember to keep letting go of any tension, to clear the mind and to keep breathing deeply into your belly. Any tension in the body or mind will affect the energy flow and will pull you out of the experience. So just relax, enjoy the moment, feel into your body and allow the energy to move through you.

PUTTING IT ALL TOGETHER

I hope that at this stage you are feeling much more embodied than you were before. If not, feel free to revisit body scans, breathing techniques and mindfulness practices that were designed to help.

But first of all, start asking yourself on a regular basis:

What am I feeling right now in my body?

Am I breathing deeply?

Where am I holding tension in my body?

What does it feel like if I let it go?

Start paying closer attention to your body while you are self-pleasuring or making love. We all habitually hold tension in our bodies during sex and in many cases we do not even realize it. See if you can identify your places of tension. Experiment with relaxing more, slowing down, noticing more in your body.

Write down your favourite embodiment technique and remember

to use it daily. It can be as simple as becoming completely still, closing your eyes and taking three deep, mindful breaths. Or it can be a body scan, a breathing technique or a simple meditation:

_____

_____

_____

_____

Make an effort to become more mindful in your life. Mindfulness is about bringing your body and mind together. If the mind is constantly racing and being distracted, you are not being mindful. Research mindfulness apps and start using one.

And finally, start making friends with your breath. Use it consciously, pay attention to the way you are breathing. Use your breath to bring more awareness, energy and vitality into your body. Practice breathing deeply, into your belly on a regular basis and keep noticing your body becoming more alive, more vibrant, more electric.

Or maybe even start seeing the breath as a lover, gently caressing your body from the inside. Delight in each breath, visualize it flowing to every part of your body, allowing more sensation and more pleasure into your life.

Part 3

GETTING OFF MINDFULLY

"I believe that one third of all individuals who are in
psychotherapy just need to learn to masturbate better. They
don't need psychotherapy. They need to explore pleasure,
intimacy, and mindfulness with a masturbation coach."

— Joseph Kramer, Ph.D.

MY HISTORY OF MASTURBATION

The first time I touched my genitals for pleasure was in my early twenties. Before that my vagina really did feel like a black hole to me – God only knew what was hidden down there, and maybe it was simply better to leave that area alone. When Ben placed my hand on my vulva for the first time, I really did not know what to do with her. Fondling her did not feel particularly ecstatic or even pleasurable to me, and it took me another few years to discover lubricants and massaging oils.

Because female genitalia are mostly inside of the body, it is much more challenging to get to know them properly, the way men are able to examine and touch their penises and testicles. And so for many years my vulva was solely a body part that I used in the toilet, without any other apparent uses or functions.

The religious upbringing was contributing a lot of shame into my relationship with my vagina. Media were sending me constant messages about her bad smell and how to fix it. Embarrassment and annoyance around my monthly menstruation was not helping, and so the way I felt about her was at best neutral and at worst – disgust.

At the age of twenty, when I got together with Ben, I started using a contraceptive pill and stayed on it for most of the following thirteen years. I enjoyed the convenience of it – protection from pregnancies, regular and easy periods, clear skin and no PMS. But in reality it completely suppressed my libido and denied me the joy of the cyclical nature of my hormonal balance. When a woman is on a pill, her hormonal levels remain the same throughout the entire cycle. This is not how female bodies are meant to operate and it is not natural.

Now I cherish my monthly hormonal changes. I celebrate my cycle and I honour my sacred time of the month – 'moon time' as the menstruation is called within spiritual communities.

And my libido can get so high! During all my years on the pill I never craved sex. My libido was non-existent, plus sex did not feel all that good. Once I quit the pill, within two months I started learning about just how horny women can get. For the first time in my life I was calling my male friends, asking them to come over because "I needed some intimacy".

In Ireland, at the age of 23, I discovered shower heads. I was having the time of my life, starting each day with an orgasm. In this water-abundant country, the Irish people did not even pay water bills back then so I felt no guilt about spending extra time in the bathroom.

A few months later I started using props. I did not have any sex toys but it turned out that kitchen utensils could be very handy, particularly when covered with olive oil. With their long and solid handles, they could fit in different places, adding extra sensations to my play time.

And so my single time was marked with solo-experimentation that pretty much completely disappeared when I was in a relationship. This is another aspect of stigmatizing masturbation in our society. For women, masturbation is seen as a last resort when they do not have a partner. And for men, the stigma around self-pleasuring reduces their self-touch to a speedy, quiet and shame-based experience which can lead to premature ejaculation and problems maintaining erection.

Self-pleasuring is a beautiful practice and should be treated as a celebration of one's body and one's sensuality. Whether single or partnered, it is essential that we have a healthy relationship with self-touch and with our body. Self-touch allows self-knowledge and a lifetime of sexual pleasure. How can you possibly expect someone to give you pleasure if you do not know how to give pleasure to yourself?

I coach my clients in their masturbation practice and give them homework that involves self-touch. I encourage exploration, curiosity and awareness as they begin to create a pleasure map of their entire body. You do know that you can feel sensual pleasure all over your body, not just in your genitals, right?

When I arrived in Australia I got my first vibrator, and a plethora of other toys followed. I felt like a kid in a candy store. I was going to sex shops and I was shopping online. I used dildos, vibrators, bullets, butt plugs, nipple clamps, outfits, bondage, handcuffs, blindfolds, different lubricants ... and the list goes on.

And as I kept playing with people, toys and my own fingers, it was still confusing me why all the sensations, all the pleasure and arousal, were gone so quickly after orgasm. It did not make any sense to me. When in the heat of the moment, I just wanted to keep going and going, planning my second and third orgasms. But once the first one was over, all the steam was gone out of my body and I was not interested in any more touch.

It took me many years to find and understand that piece of the puzzle.

Masturbation coaching

Many people restrict their masturbation practice to their genitals alone, but that is an extremely limited way to self-pleasure. Your entire body is an erogenous zone, and giving yourself a full-body sensual massage can add significantly to the amount of pleasure you experience.

One of the biggest tragedies in our modern world is the disconnection between our genitals and our heart. Our sexual energy is naturally meant to rise up through our body; it is meant to reach the heart space and then go even higher, to the head and beyond. Our sexual energy is meant to fill and nurture our entire being. But the way we usually masturbate is not allowing that to happen.

Many young men are forced to rush their masturbation practice. The fear of getting caught and embarrassed is a very real component of self-touch for many. And so we go straight for the genitals and make sure to orgasm as quickly as possible. We learn to tense up our legs and to hold our breath in order to bring ourselves to climax faster.

Locked in the genital area and unable to flow anywhere else, the erotic charge soon becomes too strong for the body to hold and ejaculation follows. This quick release can feel very pleasurable and there is nothing wrong with enjoying it. But compared to what is possible for our bodies, this kind of orgasm is a sneeze-like experience as compared to a volcanic eruption. I am not going to tell you to stop enjoying the sneeze. But I would like to ask: would you like to experience the volcano as well?

The way you masturbate wires your brain about how you are going to have sex. And this is extremely important to keep in mind when you self-touch. A woman needs you to last long enough in order for her to have a deeply satisfying experience. But if year after year you are training your body to reach a release quickly, your staying power will start to reduce. So think and decide: what kind of sexual experiences do you want to have? What does mind-blowing sex look like to you? What kind of erotic experiences do you want to share with your partner?

Once you are clear on that, ponder the following questions.

How do you masturbate?

Do you always touch yourself the same way?

How long do you last?

Exercise:

Start to introduce variety into your self-touch. Include your entire body in your practice. Slow down and use your breath consciously. Give yourself a loving self-massage while breathing deeply into your belly. Make sure to stay present with the breath, particularly when you move on to genital touch. Deep breath will keep you present and will support you in moving your sexual energy away from the genital area.

Slow down your touch. Use your non-dominant hand for a change. Do not chase any outcome, simply focus on the pleasure you are feeling in each moment. Whenever you get close to orgasm, stop the touch, relax your body and take a few deep, conscious breaths. Feel the arousal spilling out into the rest of your body and whenever you are ready, go back to self-touch.

The longer you make it last, the more intense the orgasm will be. Time spent stimulating yourself allows enough erotic charge to build up in your body to create a much more fulfilling and satisfying experience that will explode not only between your legs but through your entire being. And this is how you create an experience that allows you to stay connected to your pleasure, energized and ready for more, instead of letting all the steam out of your body and disconnecting from your sensual self.

And if you can relax your body and particularly your genitals during orgasm itself, the experience will knock your socks off!

SELF-PLEASURING – BUT WITH OTHERS

The week-long training in New Zealand's bush kept pushing me beyond my limits, and in many cases I indeed wondered whether I could actually keep participating in all the activities. Except for the peer pressure that I was feeling, there was absolutely no requirement to conform and you could sit out any or all of the activities. But considering all the time, effort and money it took me to get there, I was definitely going to get as much value out of my stay as I could.

The first evening we were divided into small groups and had to strip naked while being witnessed by others. We also had to talk to our naked bodies lovingly, embracing both their beauty and imperfections. I must admit that I was shocked and extremely nervous about this ritual but as others kept standing up and getting naked in front of me, eventually I also gathered the courage to be witnessed by them in return.

What was in fact happening was that as we were taking our clothes off, years of societal conditioning were being stripped off us at the same time. In our Western culture nudity is extremely sexualized and even demonized. In most places it is illegal to be naked in public.

Our society is sending us strong messages that it is wrong and improper to be nude. That there is something inherently bad about our bodies, and that we need to cover them up. But in the face of my new experiences, I could not help but ask – why? Why is society willing to persecute me if I ever fail to wear enough clothes?

Within just one day of seeing my new friends enjoying pure and unashamed nudity in our bush retreat, it became absolutely normal and natural for us to be naked. Some people wore clothes, some did not. Some people went walking in the bush naked, some people participated in the ongoing events naked. Strangely enough there was nothing sexual about it. There was no fear of being assaulted or embarrassed in our group. In fact, it felt absolutely natural and freeing to just be your nude self, stripped of any programming that society imposes on us.

And I loved it!

"And what about the children?" – I hear you ask. Yes, I wondered about that as well. After all, I would not want to traumatize any innocent young beings with my exposed body. But when you think about it, babies are not offended by nudity. In fact, it is us – adults – who program them to fear it. Children raised in households where parents walked around naked have a healthy relationship with their bodies. And there is no way that nudity would upset them as it is seen as normal and healthy.

That week in New Zealand brought many more challenges to my Catholic upbringing and to my beliefs about norms, sexuality and interactions with others.

On the third night, the assistants laid mattresses down all over the floor in the hall where we were all meeting together. Next we were given bottles of massaging oil and instructions about the soon to begin group self-pleasuring ritual.

Oh boy! If being naked together was challenging, how was I going to do with touching myself intimately in front of others? There was only one way to find out.

I took off my sarong and made myself comfortable in my space. I started by caressing my entire body, delighting in the softness of my skin. I allowed my body to move; I allowed little moans to escape my lips. I kept looking for all the delicious spots on my body – the back of my neck, the sides of my breasts, my inner arms and thighs, my belly and ankles. When I felt ready, I moved on to my vulva. I oiled her lovingly and started to massage her gently. I was waiting to become aroused but not much was happening. I was enjoying my touch but started to get a little frustrated that I could not build up a lot of sexual energy. I really wanted to orgasm.

And then I realized that I was anxious. Everybody around seemed to be completely focused on themselves but I still worried that someone might be watching me. I felt embarrassed and silly for feeling so but I could not help it. After a while I gave up my efforts to orgasm and just tried to relax and enjoy any pleasure that I was feeling. Orgasmic sounds made by others around me were stressing me and I felt that I was missing out on this party. Only the next day I learned that I was not the only one struggling in there.

Self-loving

The best thing that I brought with me out of that bush retreat was a new found love for my body. I learned all the ways that my body speaks to me and I started to listen. I listen to my pleasure and to my discomfort. I listen to any tension, to my relaxation and to a variety of sensations that my body uses to communicate with me. I left New Zealand feeling very raw, connected and very authentic.

I learned that my body is perfect just the way it is and that I do not need to purchase anything in order to make it better. I stopped watching TV years ago, and I refuse to be fed negative messages about the look, smell, taste or feel of my body

We all would benefit from a little more self-loving. You simply cannot delve deeply into your full sexual potential if you feel estranged from your body. If you dislike it, you will subconsciously try to disconnect from it and that will limit the level of pleasure you can feel.

Exercise:

I would like to invite you to stand naked in front of a full-length mirror. This can be very challenging for many people but please do give it a try. And then look – really look – at yourself. What do you see? What do you look at first? How do you feel about what you see?

The gaze first goes into the part of our body we dislike the most. So take a deep breath and look again. Allow your sight to wander all over your body. What parts do you love? Which parts are just ok? Where do you see the most beauty? Take it all in without any negative judgement.

And now think about how amazing your body is! It has carried you through years of experiences, adventures, maybe accidents and sicknesses. And it always recovered, it got better and you survived. Maybe you even have scars to prove it.

Think about all the pleasure your body has been giving you all your life. Think about your skin and how sensitive it is to touch.

Think about the way your body feels when you hold a loved one. When you make love. When you get a massage. When you work out. When you eat a delicious meal. When you kiss and cuddle your partner.

When you look at your body again, do it with love, with appreciation and with gratitude. Embrace your body with love, the way you would hold a loved one. Touch yourself soothingly, kindly. I promise that this shift of attitude will make a big difference in the way you experience pleasure.

MOTHER AYA

Not so long ago the world was taken by a storm of shamanic herbs capable of inducing psychedelic states of awareness for the purpose of healing a wide range of ailments, both physical and psychological. I had heard about Ayahuasca many times before I finally experienced its magic on me. I kept bumping into articles about it, and speaking to people who had drunk it and my curiosity kept growing.

I had many fears about it, particularly after reading about cases of people who ended up with serious mental issues after participating in a ceremony. I held my sound mind in high regard and was not ready to risk it. But after doing much research and seeking personal recommendations, I finally made all the arrangements and found myself at an unfamiliar venue. Surrounded by people I did not know, I was finding comfort in one friend who was there with me and who kept smiling at me with encouragement.

The ceremony started in the evening after a six hour fast. I was surprised to realize that I did not feel hunger, which was very strange considering my fast metabolism. After a beautiful opening ritual, the shaman started pouring us the drink, which did not taste nearly as bad as I expected. After drinking it, I settled in my space and waited to meet the spirit of the plant, referred to as the Mother. Nothing happened for about half an hour, during which time I kept myself occupied fearing two extreme-case scenarios – that nothing would happen at all or that my body would react so strongly, I would go through a living hell.

The Mother arrived after half an hour and I started having intense visions. First I saw an extremely colourful room and then other images flooded my mind – they were changing very quickly. Almost immediately I felt paralysed and started suffocating. I had trouble catching my breath and wanted to get outside to get some fresh air. At the same time I could not even raise my hand to ask for help, and I started to panic. I just wanted this thing out of my system but I was aware that I was facing a journey of at least four hours. Unable to move, I remembered the advice I received before to surrender to the process. I was told that the more I resisted, the harder it would be. I started repeating in my head frantically 'I am willing, I am willing, I am willing …'. I kept going until I was able to breathe normally again. I started yawning, giggling and crying. All were part of the purging process, I was told before. I remembered a few people telling me earlier that their first journey with the Mother was really gentle. This was anything BUT gentle! I kept giggling … I became aware that I would need to vomit soon, but the bucket at the end of my mat seemed so far away, I was not sure if I had it in me to reach it.

As my intense and very colourful hallucinations continued, I met a few dark beings from a different dimension. They seemed truly surprised by our low vibrational, material reality. They pointed out just how bad it felt to be in this world and I agreed, laughing out loud. Yes, I definitely preferred the world of spirit, love, light and high vibration!

At some point I also saw myself drifting in black space – very calm and safe.

I finally reached for the bucket. At the same time I feared that the purging process might give me diarrhoea (we were told that it happens). How was I going to make it to the toilet if reaching the end of my mat was such a challenge? The entire time I continued with my mantra: 'I am willing, I am willing, I am willing, why is it so freaking hard? I am willing, I am willing ...'

I managed to keep the drink down for about an hour before the physical purging started. I put my head in the bucket and when I looked up again, I saw three people helping me. One was handing me a clean bucket, another one was passing me some toilet paper and a third one was tying my long hair back. I was grateful for the help, but at the same time my body felt as if I had a very high fever. My mind and body seemed really slow to react; I felt intensely sick, hardly understanding what was going on around me. I had a faint realization that I was the first person in the group to start purging as I had not heard anyone else being sick before me.

At the same time I was experiencing very painful tummy cramps. I was guessing my body was telling me to eat something but I had no choice but to suffer through them and to ask the Mother to heal the pain. I asked her to give me sexual healing as well. That was my main intention for the evening – to finally let go of all the hurt, tension and pain caused by sex. I felt the energy of the Mother entering my yoni gently; it felt nice, extremely soothing ...

I made sure I remained extremely open the entire time, that I surrendered as much as possible. With the 'I am willing' mantra in my mind, I put my head in the bucket again. The rescue team was there in no time and I received a fresh bucket promptly. A short while later, during my third purge, the shaman came over and started hitting my back with feathers. He later told me that once I finished the purging, I raised my head up with the biggest smile on my face. He also told me that I released a huge amount of past trauma out of my body. I guess this is why it felt so bad …

After about an hour of purging, I sat up feeling much better, much healthier, and very clear in my mind. I thought that the journey was over and looked around at other people, deep in their experiences. As I felt weak after all the purging, I leaned back against the wall and closed my eyes again to rest. And then I saw her face. She was very beautiful, seemed a bit older than me, in her late 30s. She kissed my lips while penetrating my yoni again. I became aware of my whole body slowly feeling more and more alive and vibrant. She held me close while caressing my face and head. As she kept penetrating my yoni – very slowly and gently – I felt my arousal building up very fast. I realized that I had never been this turned on in my entire life as she kept making beautiful, tantric, sweet love to me. It was slow, almost still, but her energy was having a strong effect on my body. She was giving me more pleasure than any man ever had and I was completely receptive to her love. I kept asking her for more – more love and more healing. I felt full of love and kept telling her that I loved her. She kept giving me more pleasure while holding me tight.

My stomach cramps came back one more time with a very strong pain, and then they stopped. I relaxed. And then she gave me orgasms. The first one definitely caught me by surprise as I could not work out what was going on in my body. I felt intense sensations in my yoni, slowly spreading out to the rest of my body. Soon my entire body was vibrating in a more intense ecstasy than I had ever felt before. I kept asking her for more and she kept giving me more. I was blissfully happy, realizing that all my previous full-body orgasms were a weak version of this new experience. The Mother took my body to a completely new level of sexual pleasure.

This phase lasted for about an hour and a half, but it felt like she was making love to me for hours. The lovemaking was gentle, sweet, sublime ... I felt completely orgasmic in my body, mind and spirit.

And then she started to slowly leave my body. She touched my third eye and it felt almost painful as she was cleansing it. I was hanging on to her with all my strength, but after that last hour she was gone and I was sitting on my mat recalling in my head the entire experience.

All the sensations felt so real, so physical, it was hard to believe that not one person touched me during the whole evening. I realized that I did surrender after all. And that the Mother dragged me through the mud before giving me the most intense erotic experience of my life. It was exactly what I needed, and I felt extremely grateful. I thought about all my anxieties about this evening and realized that the actual experience was much worse than anything I feared. And then also much better than I could have ever asked for ...

Next we were all invited to have soup and toast and I finally realized just how famished I was. Bread and veggie soup at around midnight were a true feast. I sat with others outside, around the fire as we started sharing. I was wondering if anybody else felt as orgasmic as me, but everybody had a completely different experience.

I could not sleep that night; I kept going over the evening in my head, wanting to retain as much detail as possible. I remembered the purging phase, the suffocating, the panic, the sickness ... I was certain then that I would never do this again ... But now, I could not wait for the next time!

Self-pleasuring ritual

I guess there was no stopping me when it came to healing my sexuality and reclaiming my body as erotic! But do not worry; you do not need to drink shamanic herbs in order to become a sex god. There are many ways to live a life full of ecstatic pleasure and connection. And I find that the most direct route to your deeply erotic self is through a regular (daily in fact) self-pleasuring practice.

I am not talking here about having a quick release – far from it. In fact, ejaculation or genital touch does not even need to be a part of it. I would like you to create a ritual each time you self-touch. It does not need to be very time consuming, but if you can spend at least half an hour a day on it, that would be amazing.

Exercise:

You are going to start by creating an intention for your practice – you can use the same one every day, or you can keep changing it. Your intention will be very personal and it might be: "to last twenty minutes without ejaculating" or "to connect with my perineum and to explore my pleasure there", or "to remain completely present with my breath", or "to masturbate without porn or fantasy", or "to bring a loving touch and attention to my testicles", or "to savour all the feelings in my body". Feel free to come up with any intention that will be appropriate to you, as it will be unique and special.

Next, take a few minutes to move and touch your entire body. You can stand, sit or you can lie down. Allow your body to move and flow with any movement that feels natural. You can shake, dance, jump or stretch. As you do it, massage and caress your entire body from head to toe. This will awaken your entire being and bring a lot of awareness and sensation into your practice.

Once your whole body is feeling alive and vibrant, connect to your breath and start breathing deeply. Remain conscious of your breath for the rest of the practice as you follow your pleasure and touch yourself in any way that you wish. This is about listening to your body, to its responses and about remaining very present. Keep your body relaxed and open. Let go of any goals. Allow the deep breath to spread your pleasure and your arousal through your entire body. You can climax if you wish, but it is not the goal of this practice.

Whenever you feel ready, lie down for a few minutes of calm integration. This is a very important step so please do not skip it. As you relax into this time of quiet enjoyment of your body, your brain is working hard creating new neural connections and installing this deeper experience of yourself into your nervous system. This means that your body is learning from it and that each time you will be able to access deeper states of embodiment and bliss.

RIDING THE EDGE

Many people do not know that there is a secret to mind-blowing, spectacular, amazing, deeply satisfying orgasms. It allows you to not only consistently reach this level of ecstatic pleasure yourself but to also give this kind of experience to your partner. This secret is called 'edging'.

My very first experience with edging took me into an orgasmic state that went way beyond my own body. As my erotic energy exploded in a deeply intense climax, my whole being started to vibrate and buzz in a full-body ecstasy. My body did not feel physical anymore. I could not even feel the mattress below me. I was just pure energy pulsating in bliss, expanding out into the Universe, connecting with all beings, nature and worlds out there. It felt like a trance; my mind was free of thought, completely immersed in the experience.

I completely lost track of time and have no idea how long I stayed there. There was no time in that place.

Since then I have taught this technique to thousands of

people in person and online. The feedback I get is consistent and inspiring – edging rocks!

When you edge on your own, you are going to start your self-pleasuring practice as usual and in any way you choose. The more present you are the better this will work, but even if you choose to initially opt for porn or fantasy, that is still ok. Try to remain present enough to monitor your level of arousal – this is important! Think of a scale of one to ten where one is not aroused at all and ten is ejaculation. Keep naming your level of arousal from moment to moment; it will help you stay aware of your level of excitement and proximity to orgasm.

Be mindful of your 'point of no return'! It is located at around level eight and as soon as you get there, your ejaculatory response will be triggered. Make sure to remain at level six or seven at most.

As soon as you reach six or seven, stop all touch, relax your body and take about ten deep breaths. If you wish, you can also add a kegel on each inhale. Kegels consist of squeezing your pelvic floor muscle, the same muscle that you use to stop the stream of urine midstream. Make sure to squeeze it on the inhale and relax it on the exhale. You will start to notice your level of excitement going down a bit. You might even start to notice tingles, shivers and other gentle sensations spreading through your body.

Whenever you are ready, you can resume touch and stimulation, bringing yourself up to level six or seven again. At that point you are going to stop again and repeat the breathing and the kegels. Keep going until you have brought yourself up and down about five times. At that stage you should be experiencing vibrations and pleasure all over your body.

As you resume stimulation again, finally allow yourself to reach an orgasm. Be prepared! This experience will feel very different to what you used to call 'orgasm' before!

Sex and mathematics

The secret behind this technique lies in simple maths – the more sexual energy you stimulate and move through your body, the more spectacular its release will be at the end. Imagine pouring water into a bucket. If you only spend a moment doing it before tipping the contents out, the splash will not be too impressive. But if you take your time and fill the bucket up to the edge, the contents will spill with an appropriate level of noise and intensity.

But that is not the end of it – as you use your breath to guide your arousal out of your genitals and into the rest of your body, some of that erotic charge will stay in your body even after the orgasm, allowing you to feel energized and refreshed, instead of drained and tired.

As you can see, remaining very aware of your level of excitement during this practice is of utmost importance and training yourself to use the scale of arousal will serve you well. Many men ejaculate early simply because they are not aware of just how aroused they are. I am sure you can recall many cases when the moment of release surprised you and maybe even disappointed you as you were keen to last longer. This technique will begin to train your body to ride the waves of sexual pleasure for as long as you want. The moment of ejaculation will become your choice and never a premature surprise.

Edging is a little more tricky when performed on a partner, and requires good communication skills.

Exercise:

When edging with a lover, ask her to signal to you the moment that she is close to coming. She can say something or even tap you on the shoulder. At that stage you will stop the stimulation and guide her to relax and to use breath and kegels to move her erotic energy away from her genitals. After about ten breaths, you can resume the stimulation and so on until you finally allow her to orgasm.

INVITING GAIA

Being a spiritual person for most of my adult life, I was craving to include something larger than myself in my masturbation practice. I wanted to appropriately celebrate my sexual energy by bringing higher forces into my bedroom. So I started to wonder what that might look like.

Having participated in many shamanic and sexual rituals before, I knew that I really enjoyed extending the invitation to spirits, angels, the Earth, Mother Nature, to the sun, moon, spirits of ancestors, etc. I definitely had a soft spot in my heart for Gaia – our planet, with all the beautiful plants and animals on it. I see her as an ultimate mother, surrounding us with unconditional love, care, warmth and nurturing. Following the guidance of one of my teachers, Janine McDonald, I visualize Gaia's womb deep inside our planet and I connect to that source of nourishment and love.

And this is what I decided to do as an opening ritual of my self-pleasuring practice. I sat down cross-legged and took a few deep breaths in order to become more centred and grounded. When I felt present in my body, I closed my eyes and visualized an energetic connection between my womb and Gaia's. On each inhale I was drawing her beautiful and potent energy up into my womb, and on each exhale I was sending my loving energy down into the Earth. Soon I found myself in a blissful meditative state and I chose to stay there for a while. When I felt ready and connected, I began to move and touch my body.

Celebrating sex

In the tantric tradition, every aspect of life is seen as sacred. In our modern world, we all seem to associate Tantra with sex, but that is only a small part of this beautiful philosophy. It is, however, easy to see why our world is becoming so fascinated with Tantra – after being repressed sexually for hundreds of years, we are finally shown an approach which claims that sex is in fact healthy, normal, natural and very, very beautiful. I think this message rings true for a huge majority of people, and so we are finally finding wholeness and fulfilment in a tantric practice.

Fortunately, you do not need to know all the details of tantric philosophy in order to enjoy its benefits in your intimate life. If you can keep your body relaxed, your mind free of distractions and your breath deep and conscious, you are on your way to experiencing a deeper level of pleasure and sensuality. If you can also create a more profound and intimate connection with your partner, you both will start experiencing sex beyond anything you have known before. But we will get to that later.

Tantra teaches us to celebrate our life, and ritualizing our experience helps to embrace that principle. Every time you create a ritual around an activity, you are in fact celebrating it. The idea here is to create an experience which is more special, sacred, even magical. And you can achieve that through taking your time and preparing properly.

Exercise:

Some men struggle with the idea of creating a magical experience just for themselves, so I would like you to imagine that in fact you are preparing to welcome a very beautiful and attractive lover into your bedroom. Start by preparing the space – clear out any clutter, air the space, make the bed. Bring in candles and incense sticks or essential oils. Beautify the space in any way that you want – maybe bring extra cushions, flowers, put on some sensual music, maybe even prepare some light snacks and drinks. Make sure that the space is warm enough so that you can be comfortable naked. See your bedroom as a temple of delight and pleasure, and prepare it accordingly.

If candles are on, you can turn off the main light in order to create a more romantic atmosphere. You are your own best lover and you deserve the best treatment!

Take a shower or a bath. Spray a beautiful perfume on your body if you wish. As you enter your sacred space, sit down on your bed and take a few moments to meditate and to become present. Simply connecting with your breath for a few minutes will be enough. Keep noticing each inhale and exhale until you feel calm and grounded.

Open your eyes and set an intention. You can invite higher forces into your space or the spirits of the land. This is completely up to you. Do whatever resonates with you and enjoy the process. Do not make it too serious and remember to have fun! Tantra is very playful, so make sure to smile at yourself often.

Begin with some movement and self-massage. If you have a

mirror in the room, perform a seductive dance for yourself. Undress slowly while touching and caressing your entire body. Hey, what do you have to lose? Nobody is watching!

Remain very conscious of your breath as you self-pleasure, and play with your sexual energy. Use edging or any other method that will allow you to last as long as you wish. Really take your time with yourself. You would not want things to end too quickly with a very special someone else, right?

End the ritual with at least a few minutes of quiet integration as you relax completely still. Savour all the pleasure in your body. There is nothing else to do here. The ritual starts with 'doing' and ends with 'being'. Allow yourself to be in bliss for as long as it feels good.

WITNESSING

It should hardly surprise me anymore that my path of sexual discovery takes me to really unusual and uncommon experiences. But witnessing a stranger self-pleasure, and then being witnessed by them in return, was something I did not see coming.

As a part of my certification in sexological bodywork with the Institute of Somatic Sexology, I needed to go through many different embodied practices, and witnessing was one of them. I had no idea what to expect or how this would go. But at this stage I was not even getting nervous anymore about all the new sexual experiences.

When Jodie turned up at my doorstep, this was our first face-to-face meeting. We were attending the same training and we decided to meet up and perform this assignment together. We had a tea and a chat before I took her to the bedroom. She was young, pretty, really nice and a little on the shy side.

Jodie decided to be witnessed first, and she put on a candle before getting undressed. We agreed to have half an hour each. She stood naked in front of the mirror and started to move in rhythm with sensual music playing softly. Her hands kept wandering up and down her gorgeous feminine body and her breath remained deep and full.

When she kneeled down on the mattress, she reached for her vulva and the speed of her breath started to increase. As her arousal kept growing, I was mind-blown by the transformation happening right in front of my eyes. This shy little girl with big glasses on her nose started to morph into a wild sex goddess full of beauty, sensuality and deep desire. Her body kept dancing her pleasure with beautiful sounds escaping her lips. I was in awe, deeply honoured to be able to witness her in this raw, ecstatic experience.

Her climax was intense, followed by a calm integration time.

After she showered and returned to the room, it was my turn to be witnessed. I removed my clothes and took a few moments to breathe and to connect to my body. After that I stood up and started to admire my body in the mirror. The thoughts of being watched by someone and having to perform in some way came and went as I decided to follow my body's impulses instead of any script my mind would come up with.

I used movement and self-touch to awaken my skin and my bodily awareness. When I laid down my touch focused more on my breasts and genitals. I was slowly stimulating my erotic energy while regulating my arousal with breath. To this day I am not certain what exactly happened there, but within ten minutes from the beginning of my practice my mind went into a trance-like state. And I had not even orgasmed yet! It was amazing and blissful. Completely free of thought, I was flowing with my body and my pleasure, completely immersed in the experience. I lost track of time as there did not seem to be any time in the place I was at.

The session took me extremely deep and I wonder how exactly being witnessed affected me that evening. Free of the anxiety I experienced in New Zealand, I was completely relaxed and able to reach a deep state of ecstatic trance. After a breathtaking climax, there was nothing else to do but lie there in a perfect peace and surrender.

Being seen

Have you ever witnessed someone else's masturbation? Have you been witnessed yourself? How do you feel about the prospect of witnessing each other? Is it scary? Exciting? Foreign?

Most people crave to be seen in their pure, raw pleasure. This experience itself can be extremely healing if you have any history of shame and guilt in your sexual life. To be lovingly held in another's full presence is an amazing gift. This is also referred to as 'holding space'. You hold space for a person when you give them your full undivided attention while they are going through their process. You are not judging them, not interrupting them in any way. You are simply being there for them. They might ask you to assist them somehow, but most likely you will just need to be present with nothing else expected of you.

Exercise:

If you have a lover, ask them if they would like to practice mutual witnessing. If you do not have one, ask a close friend. You can contact a Tantra practitioner if you prefer to be witnessed by a stranger. You can also set up a camera and record your session. Watching yourself masturbate can be a very profound experience as it will reveal to you new things about your sexuality – things that you might not have been aware of before.

If you do the witnessing with another person, make sure to

communicate well about what it is that you want to achieve. Make it clear that it is not an invitation to have sex or to be touched by the witness. Explain to them your intention and make sure to answer any questions they might have.

BACK DOOR TO HEAVEN

There is no way of completing this section without discussing the anus. Anal pleasure is an often ignored aspect of our sexuality. Our society has multiple hang-ups when it comes to anal touch. The main concerns that are raised in my sessions are: shame, hygiene, fear of pain and homosexual tendencies.

A majority of straight men consider anal touch wrong. They are afraid that if they do enjoy it, it will mean that they are gay. From peer pressure to messages received from the media, there is a strong expectation that men are masculine – meaning straight, strong and emotionally stable. They are told from an early age that 'boys do not cry'. They are advised to 'man up' and to 'not be a girl'. Being called a 'pussy' is strongly offensive to the masculine ego. And so, men keep rising to the macho model, locking their pelvises, chronically clenching their anuses and disconnecting from their emotions.

Let me tell you something about your anus – it hosts a high density of nerve endings, making it a very potent place for both pleasure and pain. And this is the case for both men and women, for people who are gay and people who are straight. I know a lot of men who enjoy anal touch while having no desire to ever be with another man. So my advice to you is: get over yourself as you are missing out!

First, stop and enquire within. What is your relationship with your anus? Do you experience pleasure there? Have you ever tried? Do you experience shame about your anal area? Do you consider anal stimulation wrong? Do you think it is painful? Have you ever experienced anal trauma through a medical procedure or uninvited touch?

Your relationship with your anus can be simple or very complex, but in either case denying its existence is not going to solve anything. Shining the light of awareness and curiosity on your back door is a wonderful start to new possibilities and a healthier relationship with your body.

Let us start with some anal anatomy. The entrance of your anus is made up of two anal sphincters. The external one is under your conscious control – you can clench it and you can relax it at will. The second one is located inside, about one centimetre deep, and is governed by subconscious parts of your brain; i.e., you cannot control it at will. Past your anal sphincters you will encounter your rectum, an area where faeces are stored right before a bowel movement. You might encounter small bits of faeces in there, so if it bothers you, it might be a good idea to do an enema before your anal play. Or you can simply use vinyl gloves.

Please be aware that anal stimulation should never be painful. If it ever is, you are doing it wrong!

Exercise

Here is what I want you to do. Start by relaxing your body and simply bringing your attention to your anus through anal breathing. On every inhale you are going to clench your anal sphincter and on every exhale you are going to relax it. Continue for a few minutes.

When you are ready, apply massaging oil to your fingers and your anus. You are going to start with an external anal massage. Most men find anal massage extremely relaxing. This is because much of the tension they had been holding there for years is finally released. Many men find it also really arousing and a great way to add a new dimension of deep pleasure into their masturbation practice.

Play with different strokes; make little circles around your anus, brush past it with one or a few fingers, keep pressing on it and releasing or use tapping. You can also reach for toys. According to Joseph Kramer, Ph.D., pressing a vibrating massager to your anus can induce states of deep bliss!

In your own time and if you are ready to do so, you can move on to internal strokes. Insert just the tip of your finger first and become familiar with your anal sphincters. You can squeeze and release the sphincter around your finger to give yourself a better understanding of your anatomy. Make sure to keep using enough oil as there is no natural lubrication in the anus.

If you are feeling a lot of tension inside, start by stretching the anus in four directions with your finger. Remember to back off if you experience any pain! You can also move your finger around, massaging the inside of the anal opening. If everything is going well so far, try to venture even deeper and explore your prostate. You might need to use a toy as it might be difficult to reach. Your prostate is located on the belly side of your rectum and it will feel very pleasurable to touch if you are aroused. You can also insert a vibrating toy inside, or use a butt plug.

See if it feels good to combine anal strokes with the stimulation of your penis. Be adventurous, be creative but also be loving and compassionate towards your body if it refuses to play at this time. Try again later – maybe run yourself a bath and try there. Do not be impatient, there is no rush.

PUTTING IT ALL TOGETHER

I hope that at this stage you are feeling informed and inspired to take your self-pleasuring practice to a new level, and to create new experiences of pleasure, intensity and depth in your life.

If not, I am going to give you a little cheat sheet with different options that I invite you to play with. In either case, please remember that there is no right or wrong way to self-pleasure. Your practice is your practice and if you feel like simply tickling your chest for half an hour, that is perfectly fine! Let go of a need for anything to happen. Delight in connecting with your body without any goals. Sometimes all I do is breathe deeply while caressing my arms. Other times I use toys and take myself on a wild ride. It is your playground and your rules!

1/ Relaxation
Once you become very aware during your self-pleasuring practice, you will start to notice that you are holding a lot of tension in your body, particularly in your pelvis. Make an effort to let it go. Relaxation is not

about being limp. It is about experiencing pleasure free of tension and energetic blockages. You can still be active and very relaxed.

Relaxation will allow your arousal to spill out of your genitals and into the rest of your body. This way, instead of experiencing genital sneezes, you will access states of full-bodied pleasure and ecstasy.

2/ Breath

We often constrict or hold the breath as we become aroused. Let go of the tension and engage deep, belly breathing throughout your practice. It will serve two purposes: keeping you present in your body (your breath will default to shallow breathing when you do not control it so make sure that you are breathing deeply and it will help your mind stay engaged and free of distractions) and spreading erotic sensations throughout your whole being.

Feel free to use a circular breath – it is a very regular, rhythmic way of breathing. The length of each inhale is approximately the same as the length of exhale, and there are no pauses between breathing in and out. So this breath is flowing smoothly, calmly, like a circle.

Play with different speeds. Slow the breath right down and notice the effects on your body. And then speed it up. Stay curious and open. But do not take it too far; if you are feeling dizzy or light headed, adjust the breath to keep yourself comfortable.

3/ Presence

Many men use porn and fantasy in order to get in the mood. There is nothing wrong with enjoying erotic imagery unless you are dependent on it for arousal. During your new masturbation practice, do your best to stay completely focused on your body. Whenever your attention wanders to the computer screen or to your imagination, it takes your awareness away from you and from sensations in your body.

If you are struggling with this, commence your practice with erotic images but once you are aroused, bring your attention back to your body. You will soon discover that mindfulness is a key to reaching depths of pleasure that are not possible when your mind is engaged elsewhere.

4/ Intention

Ritualize your practice and start with a clear intention. Feel into your body and decide what it is that it needs for a much fuller, more embodied experience.

You can also call in any forces into your bedroom that resonate with you. Long before people worshipped a God, for thousands of years they worshipped a Goddess – a feminine force behind all creation, birthing the whole Universe in the container of consciousness of Her beloved.

Try calling in the Goddess and see how it feels.

5/ Curiosity

When you first learned to masturbate, you were most likely using fast, efficient strokes that brought you to orgasm quickly. Do you still touch yourself the same way?

Embrace and explore new ways to touch your body. Do not go for the same old strokes again and again. Slow down your touch, use the other hand, play with massaging oils and toys.

Give yourself permission to make sounds! Explore anal touch. Do not be afraid to try something new!

6/ Take care of your body

This is an important and often overlooked aspect of sexuality. You will obtain much more enjoyment out of your body if you take good care of it. This means exercise and a healthy diet. Take care of any health issues and make sure to drink plenty of water.

Many men spend hours every day sitting down – at the computer desk or on the couch at home. This leads to tension in the pelvis and energetic blockages in the anus. If you want to experience your body as full of vitality and aliveness, you need to provide it with appropriate movement and nutrition. Reduce your use of alcohol, give up cigarettes and fast food. Opt for wholefoods and home cooked meals. You might need to reduce coffee too! And then watch your body opening up to more and more pleasure.

Part 4

ENJOY RECEIVING

"Open your hands, if you want to be held."

— Rumi

FOUR TYPES OF TOUCH

Learning about Dr. Betty Martin's Wheel of Consent[10] was very eye-opening to me. I had never before analysed all the different inter-actions and energy exchanges that were happening in sex between me and my lovers. We were in bed together touching each other, what more was there to it than that?

The way Betty mapped out touch and consent gave me a new understanding of not only what happens between lovers, but also why my previous sex life was riddled with so much frustration and discontentment.

According to Betty's wheel, there are four types of touch possible – giving, receiving, taking and allowing. Each kind of touch has a healthy expression and a shadow side. The touch enters the shadow when it is still happening despite the fact that you or the other person does not want it anymore. It is a touch without consent.

When you are giving, you are touching the other person for their pleasure only. You are being of service to them. So this happens when you are giving your lover a massage, oral sex, when you caress them, etc. You can, of course, enjoy being of service and pleasuring them. But the intention behind the touch is to give pleasure, not to receive it. You are giving from the place of generosity. The shadow side of giving will make you feel like a martyr; maybe you are the one who is always giving, and the resentment begins to build up within you. In the long run, giving from the place of shadow will make you feel burnt out and depleted.

When you are receiving, the other person is performing the giving touch for your enjoyment. So this happens when you are receiving a massage or erotic touch from them. You can kick back, relax and simply surrender to the pleasure. You are benefiting from your lover's actions and you are feeling gratitude. The shadow side of receiving is being lazy, selfish or even exploiting your partner. Are you the one doing all the receiving in bed? If so, your lover might start to feel resentful.

When you are taking, you are touching your lover for your own enjoyment. We usually have negative associations with taking from others, but it can be a very valid and beautiful way to touch when done in full integrity, without abusing the other person. In fact, I love it when my lovers touch me for their pleasure. I love feeling their desire for my body and how they cannot get enough of me. In my experience men usually take when it comes to breasts. They are absolutely mesmerized by them and cannot help but touch and fondle them. The shadow side of taking is rape and assault. This is a very serious shadow which can definitely negatively influence our associations with taking.

And finally, when you are allowing, your partner is touching you for their own benefit and pleasure. This happens when you surrender to their touch, when you allow them to 'have their way with you' in bed. In fact, most women love to surrender to the masculine touch while they are being lovingly ravished. But if you do not give consent to the touch, you will enter the shadow side where you will find yourself feeling like a victim, used or resentful.

When I looked back at my own life before Tantra, I realized that I was always either giving or allowing. The other two quadrants of the wheel were completely foreign to me. I never felt like I was receiving or taking. I did not even really know back then how to take! When in bed, I was always very focused on my partner's pleasure, making sure that he was having a great experience. My own pleasure was somehow being overlooked. I am sure that my lovers had good intentions and that in many cases they felt like they were giving to me. But because of lack of communication or poor lovemaking skills, I was not actually receiving pleasure from their touch and was stuck in the allowing quadrant – or even in its shadow side. So we were creating this unhealthy dynamic and we did not know what to do about it.

Intention behind the touch

Distinguishing between different types of touch during lovemaking can be tricky, and it is not always completely black and white which kind of touch is happening. When you are kissing each other, are you giving or taking? When she is caressing your chest, are you receiving or allowing? Look at the intention behind the touch. Are you doing something because it feels good to you, or because you know how much she loves it and you want to give her pleasure? You can even have a chat in bed, during or after your lovemaking experience, identifying who did what and in which quadrants you both were during the touch. I am sure you will discover new things about your lover if you can both communicate about your experience honestly and openly.

The main thing to remember is that in order to have a well-balanced and satisfying sex life, you need to incorporate all four aspects of touch into your experience. You need to do a bit of giving and some receiving, and some taking and some allowing. If you remain in only some parts of the wheel you will eventually enter the shadow side, causing issues and resentment between you and your lover.

Exercise:

So now it is time to look at your own life and your own experience in bed. Where do you find yourself mostly when it comes to the Wheel of Consent? Which quadrants would you like to visit more often? Which ones less often? Do you ever find yourself in the shadow, and when?

Allow this information to give you a new insight into your intimate relationships and let it guide you to more pleasure, more satisfaction and more mutual nurturing in bed.

SACRED SPOT MASSAGE

Looking back at my weeklong training in New Zealand, the absolutely most challenging experience I had there was receiving a Sacred Spot massage. Sacred Spot massage is a beautiful experience of sexual healing and deepening your connection with your erotic self. It can potentially draw years of trauma, pain and abuse out of your genitals – when performed by a knowledgeable and professional practitioner. However, in New Zealand we – the inexperienced participants – were performing it on each other.

A Sacred Spot session consists of an internal massage, with a series of points being massaged and held in order to let go of tension and emotional blockages in our genitals. For women the Sacred Spot is accessed through the vagina and for men – through the anus. It is truly mind blowing how much we can hold in our genitals. We are holding on to our past trauma, to shame, to guilt, to embarrassment. We are holding on to anger, sadness, grief and frustration.

Very early in our lives we internalize the messages about sex and genitals that our environment sends us. It can even happen quite unintentionally when our parents cringe in disgust while changing our nappies. After all, it feels so good to make a poo but when it causes a negative reaction in the caregiver, an internal conflict follows and we begin to clench the anus.

When kids are being potty trained before they are ready, this will in most cases result in chronic tension and potentially ongoing constipation issues, due to forcibly pushing down on their genitals.

When adults make jokes at kids' nudity or angrily urge them to cover up, kids start to associate their bodies and genitals with something bad and improper.

When parents tense up and feel awkward or even panic at a sex scene accidentally popping up on the TV screen, children learn that sex is wrong and scary.

When a young man ejaculates too early or is unable to produce an erection when with a girl, she might shame him with her reaction or might even sleep with one of his friends, causing him to feel inadequate and not good enough.

This early in my journey of sexual awakening, I was terrified at the prospect of having my genitals touched by a stranger, and I actually had a cry before the Sacred Spot ritual began. I knew that I could back out, but what was the point of me being there if I was just going to sit back and watch without participating? Only I wondered if there really was not any simpler way to heal my traumas.

The process of pairing up men and women for the evening was very beautiful. Men and women were in separate rooms and we were given two trays with tokens on them. There were two of each token and they were all items coming from the bush – two matching leaves, two matching flowers, two matching branches, pine cones, stones, etc.

The tokens were divided between the trays so that there was one item of each pair on each tray. Men were given one tray, and women the other. Next, we had to pick an item each and then go and find our partner with the matching token.

Still shaken and scared, I was waiting for the tray to reach me and when it did, it tipped slightly to one side as it was passed to me by one of the girls. I caught it right in time and as I did, one of the tokens fell into my hand. I looked at it in surprise and decided to keep it. It seemed that the Universe heard my crying and was giving me a helping hand with my choice.

I found my partner for the evening and we started with a chat in order to agree on boundaries, and the course of the massage itself. Stewart was in his mid-forties and very caring. In fact, he was so gentle, loving and kind with me that during the massage he took my body into a deeply healing process. I later learned that he had actually had a lot of previous experience with massage.

I laid down on my front and he started by relaxing me with his touch. I was loving all the strokes, and I allowed my body to drop into a state of deep relaxation and surrender. When he asked me to turn over, I was barely able to move! As he gently worked on the front of my body, I suddenly found myself in a state of trance – I was losing touch with the physical reality I was in, and it felt very blissful. It was similar to having an Ayahuasca journey or tripping on acid, but much gentler.

As I was peacefully floating in my altered state, a strong wave of energy shot through my body bringing me back from my bliss. Few more waves followed and they were so intense, I could not help but scream out loud each time. At one point, I saw the face of my lover and I reached out to touch him. He was not there, but I knew that somehow he was with me.

Nothing like that had ever happened to me before, and I had no script to guide me through this new and surprising experience. Stewart remained very present with me, holding space for me without interrupting my experience. He was not asking any questions but his hands were reassuringly holding my body, letting me know that he was there and that I was safe. I was very grateful to him and thanked him from the bottom of my heart as he was holding me tight after the massage was over.

Surrendering to touch

Receiving touch can be a very challenging experience, particularly for men. The nature of masculine energy is to give, to be active, to move towards a goal, to be dynamic. The nature of feminine energy is to surrender, to receive and to dance in her creative essence while being held in the presence and consciousness of her partner. I do not mean to say that all men and all women are like that. There are men who are well-connected to their feminine side and who are very comfortable surrendering and receiving. And there are women who are quite masculine and who enjoy taking charge and being in control.

So where are you on this spectrum? And how do you feel about receiving?

Many men I work with tell me how uncomfortable they feel about being in the receptive role. How much they want and need to touch, to give. And I guide them to explore and experience the other end of the spectrum. There is something very beautiful and healing about simply surrendering to touch, whether you are a male or a female. Think about all the enjoyment that you get from giving pleasure to your partner. Would you not like for her to have the same experience while she is giving to you?

From time to time, just for kicks, let go of the need to be masculine. You do not need to keep proving your masculinity every single day for the rest of your life. Just explore receiving. Allow yourself to be spoiled, pampered, treated, caressed, enticed, teased and pleasured by a loving partner. I think that you might like it!

COCONUT OIL BLISS

They say you never forget your first time. I will definitely never forget my first tantric time!

I met Jonathan at my very first conscious sexuality conference. As a newly baked Tantra teacher, I decided that I needed to attend all the industry events I could find. I wanted to know who was who, I wanted to network and meet other teachers and practitioners. And I wanted to learn. I wanted to know exactly who does what, how and why.

Jonathan was one of the presenters and a very experienced Tantra practitioner. I knew of him before I arrived there and was hoping for an opportunity to speak to him. I did not have to wait long; in the morning of our second day he was standing right there in front of me outside one of the conference rooms.

I approached him and we had a lovely chat. He was not only tall, dark and handsome but also very kind, warm and caring. We bumped into each other a few more times during the conference, and it was fairly obvious that there was sexual attraction between us.

We did not get a chance to spend any time together after hours but we did stay in touch afterwards, and two months later Jonathan came over for a visit. Once we got a chance to really connect and talk, it became very clear to me that we were very different and that we wanted different things in life. But despite the lack of any romantic connection, the sexual spark was still there and we could not wait to have sex.

I had heard and read stories of him as a lover, and was very curious about him. We quickly developed a lovely friendship and he always treated me with warmth and love, so it was very easy for me to surrender to his touch and his penis.

As is usually the case with hype and sensationalized stories, the actual experience did not fully match my expectation, but Jonathan still blew my mind in different ways. First of all, he gave me the most intense experience of masculine presence that I had ever had up to that point. He did not become lost in his own experience and pleasure even for one moment, remaining closely connected to me and my body. I felt held, embraced and deeply loved the entire time. He kept saying the most beautiful things to me and I was happily surrendering to his loving.

He showed me just how different sex feels when the man is not chasing his ejaculation. In fact, he hardly felt the need to release inside of me at all, which gave our lovemaking a beautiful dimension of gently flowing together, of slowing down and savouring the experience, of being *in* sex instead of doing it.

He showed me how I can control my own energy in order to support the man in retaining his semen. Many women unconsciously pull the semen out of the man in a biological need to be impregnated. Once the couple becomes aware of this dynamic, they can take control of it and the woman can use her awareness and her energetic flow to help the man last as long as he wants.

And he showed me all the different uses of coconut oil in bed. In fact, I still recommend coconut oil to all of my clients as a great alternative to lubricants. The problem with lubricants is that they contain chemicals and usually keep drying up, requiring multiple applications. Our genitals are very sensitive and our skin is permeable, meaning that it has the ability to absorb whatever is applied on top of it. A woman's vagina is particularly receptive and can draw the nasty chemicals into the woman's system.

Coconut oil is very natural, contains no chemicals, is moisturising, anti-inflammatory and overall very good for our skin and body. It can be safely applied to genitals and will not dry up or need multiple applications. It is also edible, which will allow you to move on to oral sex safely if you wish for that to happen. The only word of caution is that any oil will break down the latex in condoms so if you are using protection, opt for a latex-free option.

Jonathan and I went through a lot of coconut oil in the space of three days. And it felt wonderful! The oil completely eliminated the painful friction that I knew so well from my previous sexual encounters. Up to that point, whenever I had sex for more than a few minutes, I always ended up sore and needed at least a day to recover. With Jonathan, we were making love for hours, two or three times a day, without any discomfort or burning in my genitals.

I still use coconut oil to this day, even though I can lubricate abundantly. It simply makes the experience easier and more enjoyable.

Feel free to experiment with other oils as well. I have heard that almond oil is pretty yummy too!

Connection through presence

How present are you as a lover? Do you reach for a fantasy as soon as you start connecting with her sexually? Are you completely absorbed in building your excitement and in pushing your body to produce a rock-hard erection as soon as possible?

Many men experience anxiety about their erections. Their level of confidence as lovers is strongly connected to their penises and their performance. In many cases this is linked to previous traumatic experiences. If your body did not act the way you wanted it to, you might have experienced shame and embarrassment because of it. Maybe you even lost a lover.

Think about it – when it comes to sex, men are under a lot of pressure. They need to produce an erection, maintain it for long enough, not lose it at any point, make sure not to ejaculate too quickly, make sure to ejaculate at the right time and make sure to ejaculate at all. This can create a high level of stress and tension in your mind and body. And guess what – tension further inhibits your ability to perform during sex!

The truth about erections

We all know that the body changes with age. The skin becomes thinner and starts to wrinkle, the digestion slows down, muscles become weaker, hair thinner, bellies rounder ... Yet we think that erections are outside of the influence of aging. They are not! A man in his thirties will discover that his body is not as prone to spontaneous erections as it was when he was a teenager or in his early twenties. He will also discover that, on occasion, he might not actually be able to have an erection when he wants to. Past the age of forty, this tendency will become even stronger as guaranteed erections become a thing of the past. He will be definitely able to have an erection, but not every single time. His erections will not be as strong anymore either.

Many men come to me asking me to help them have a rock-hard erection for hours. And as much as I can help them strengthen their erections, it is a myth and an unrealistic expectation to be this hard for this long.

In my experience as a woman and as a Tantra practitioner, erections come and go. Making love for hours does not mean penetrating her with a rock-hard penis the entire time. I actually think that it would be quite boring if it was the case!

In Tantra, sex does not equal intercourse. Penetration is just one of the aspects of lovemaking. Tantric sex consists of connecting intimately, of becoming present together, of setting an intention, of breathing in sync, of caressing, touching, kissing, circling energy between your bodies, using erotic massage, opening your hearts and delving deep into each other. It is a playful connection of two bodies, two minds, two hearts and two souls. It is a deep exploration of each other in the space of a sacred union. It is a session of worship and of honouring each other's body. It is a sensual ritual of intimate connection without a script or a goal.

As Deej Juventin from the Institute of Somatic Sexology taught me, once you start to grow older "it is not just about your hard cock anymore".

In your teenage years and early twenties, your body is biologically primed to produce an offspring, so erections are strong, frequent and easy. You can ejaculate often and the refractory period is reasonably short. Your body's focus is in your pants to the point where it can get annoying.

With age, this focus shifts to your heart. Your body does not want to connect with a woman only through an erection anymore. You start to appreciate the finer aspects of your relationship with her, you start to look for that special spark in her eye, you start having deep and meaningful conversations with her and you actually enjoy them instead of simply waiting to have sex with her. You take her dancing, and delight in watching her body twirl and bend in a sensual joy of movement and flow.

So please stop worrying so much about your erection and your performance. If she walks out of your life because you did not have a rock-hard erection for an hour, she was not worth your time or your affection.

Exercise:

Start cultivating the quality of presence in your intimate encounters. Remain completely mindful and connected to your lover instead of disappearing in your head. Hold her with full awareness, give her one hundred percent of your attention. Let her know with your poise that you are her warrior, her protector, that you are cherishing your time together and that you will not abandon her to pursue a fantasy. Not many women in our society have experienced this level of presence. If you can do that for her, you will be that one lover she will never forget.

SOBBING IN ECSTASY

Anthony was a friend of mine for almost a year before he finally brought up the subject of the sexual tension present between us. I loved him like a brother and was not fussed about having sex with him since I had other lovers in my life. Fortunately, I was unaware of how good a lover he was; otherwise I would have begged him for sex much sooner!

Once we became lovers, things quickly got complicated and our sex affair did not last long. But when we did have sex, it was an out of this world experience.

He was very present, amazing at taking his time with me and a master teaser. I loved surrendering to his masculine strength and his raw passion. He was confident, creative and he knew exactly how to pull my hair back to shock me into submission without causing me any pain.

Making love to him felt easy and his cock inside me felt divine. His penetration was slow, deliberate, unhurried. He was able to be completely still inside me while at the same time sending my body on a rollercoaster of energetic ecstasy. His penis was so conscious and present that he helped me release a lot of emotional pain out of my yoni.

I cried every time we made love as his cock was lovingly dissolving places of tension and grief in my vagina. And he knew how to hold space for my emotional releases – with presence and care. When the body is touched with awareness and love, when you feel safe and held, all the suppressed emotions, all the unconscious clenching can finally become processed and let go. As the wave of sadness, frustration, anger or fear starts to leave your body, it is often manifested in tears, screams or body shakes.

Anthony was very comfortable at receiving as well. While strongly connected to his masculine essence, he was still able to relax and ask me for what he wanted. And I was delighted to give it to him. Once you know exactly what your lover wants, it is so easy to pleasure them!

We talked often during sex and the communication was allowing us to fine tune the experience for maximum pleasure and connection. I never felt used by him, and our exchange was balanced and healthy.

I started to wonder why it is so hard for so many people to ask for what they want in bed. And soon I came to a realization that many people do not know what it is that they want. We are usually aware of what we do not like, but we are not so good at pinpointing what we do desire.

Active receiving

Sexual communication is an important skill, and there is simply no way to have consistently great sex if you cannot talk about it. We all have different needs and our needs change, often daily. Many people assume that their partner should know how to touch them. But how would they know if you never tell them? We are not mind readers and we need guidance in order to bring each other the most bliss.

Do you recall ever touching your partner while she was just lying there without any reaction? Were you asking yourself how much she was actually enjoying your touch, and if she was at all? Would you not have appreciated some feedback so that you knew that you were on the right track? Even a moan or a delicious stretch would sometimes have been enough. And a few words of appreciation or constructive feedback – even better!

And now think about all the different times when your lover was pleasuring you and it was good but would have been better if she did it a little differently – if she adjusted the pressure, speed or location of her touch. But you did not say anything because you were worried that she would feel hurt or upset by your comment. She was making an effort for you after all, and you did not want to criticize her.

But if the situation was reversed and you were caressing her while she was more tolerating your touch than actually enjoying it – would you not like to know about that? And would it not be good if she said "that feels so nice darling, and how about you do this a little firmer, that would feel even nicer!"

Start to use language in sex; it can actually be a potent aphrodisiac as you are whispering words of passion into your lover's ear. Or when you are telling her how much you are enjoying her touch and what you would like her to do to you next. Or telling her what you are about to do to her and enquiring about her feedback.

Whenever you are asking for something, make sure to start with a positive encouragement before making your request. "I really like what you are doing and could you please give me some oral love" sounds better than "I want you to suck my cock" or sticking your penis in her face.

Exercise:

So here is a fun exercise I would like you to play with. It is a practice of active receiving which will help you develop a deep sense of what it is your body wants and how to ask for it. You will need assistance from a lover, friend or a professional practitioner. The rules are simple – your partner in this game is only allowed to touch you in exactly the way that you requested.

You can lie down on your front or on your back, whichever you prefer. Take a few deep breaths, allow yourself to become present in your body. Try to really feel into your body, listening to its needs and wants. Keep playing with the circular breath or any other breathing technique you like. And once you are ready, start making requests. If your partner is ever uncertain about the touch you are after, they can ask you to clarify or even to show them what it is that you mean. Just keep guiding them. This session is for you, so do not be shy to ask for exactly what you want!

Active communication

Here is an example of what the communication during a session of active receiving might look like:

Receiver: Could you please start lightly caressing my body from head to toe?

Giver: Sure. Is this the pressure you mean?

R.: A little softer, please.

G.: Thank you. How is that?

R.:   Perfect.

G.:   Would you like me to include genitals in this touch?

R.:   No, not yet, thank you for asking.

G.:   No problem.

R.:   And could you please now concentrate your touch on my chest while gently pinching my nipples?

G.:   Did you want the same pressure on your chest as before?

R.:   No, I would like you to use your entire palm and a firmer pressure.

G.:   Thank you. How is that pressure on your nipples?

R.:   It's lovely, thank you.

R.:   And could you please now place one hand on my heart and the other hand on my genitals?

G.:   Could you please show me the kind of pressure you would like me to use?

R.:   (pressing Giver's hand to his chest) Like that.

G.:   Thank you.

Etc.

It is also a good idea to make some agreements at the beginning of the session – how long the session will last, whether there are any areas of your body you do not want touched, whether you are anticipating that you might change your mind about these areas, whether you are going to ask for genital touch and if that is ok with the giver, etc.

You will find that each time you play with active receiving, asking for what you want will become easier and easier. You will also become much more connected to your body and your sensual and erotic desires.

It is so easy to get lost and distracted while so much is happening during sex. Active receiving allows you to slow down, connect to your body, listen and then express what you want. These are all very useful skills in great lovemaking!

ANAL SURPRISE

I have performed more prostate massage sessions with my clients than I can count or recall. Each session is very unique as everybody has a different relationship with their anus and a different level of shame, discomfort, numbness, pleasure or openness within it.

When working with clients, I am not attached to any outcome; I simply guide them with my voice and with my touch, and assist them in any process that is meant to happen for them. I never really know how the session will go, but I trust my intuition and follow the responses of the body of my client. When it comes to any physical touch in my practice, being present, open and loving are of utmost importance.

I see every part of our body as precious and sacred. I consider every single body I work on as a temple and treat it with respect and reverence. I feel honoured that my clients trust me enough to allow me to touch the most fragile and sensitive parts of their erotic anatomy. I have guided many people on the road of reclaiming their body as sensual and ecstatic and I have witnessed many somatic openings.

The most profound experiences of deepening one's erotic awareness and pleasure usually happen during sessions of anal and prostate massage. As the man finally lets go of all the limiting beliefs about his anus and of the tension he had been holding there for years, a journey of deep healing and connection can begin.

When Bob came to see me for a session, he was in his late sixties and had never experienced any anal stimulation in his life. His doctor recommended that he see a Tantra practitioner because his libido was extremely low and he had not been sexually active for many years. Bob was seeing different therapists and was slowly getting better; however, he still needed some support on his way to reconnecting with his sexuality and arousal.

During our initial chat I asked whether he would be open to experiencing anal touch. He answered that he had full trust in me and that I could do whatever I wanted to. I smiled at this response and we began the massage.

I taught him how to breathe and I guided him through a mindfulness meditation. I helped him relax and when he was ready, I started working on his anus. During the external massage I kept watching his face and body closely, looking for any signs of discomfort, but he was actually responding really well – he was getting aroused and kept making satisfied grunts and comments. When I inserted the tip of my finger in his anus and mapped his anal sphincter area, I remained very present and kept checking in with him, but he was having a great time!

I continued with the internal and prostate massage. I made sure to keep building his awareness of his anal area as this was his first ever proper experience of anal touch. When we finished I guided him to a few minutes of calm integration, but he could not wait to tell me all about his experience!

Bob called the session ecstatic and advised me that he had never experienced such intense pleasure in his life. As he kept joyfully and excitedly sharing with me, I also learned that he would never admit to anybody that he allowed someone to put a finger in his anus. Or that he enjoyed it!

He returned to see me a few more times, each time reaching a deeper and deeper level of embodiment and pleasure.

Taboo of the anus

Being penetrated by another person can make one feel extremely vulnerable. When you add to this a ton of negative conditioning around anuses that we grow up with in our society, you can start to comprehend why men clench and protect their back sides so much. Notice how you are placing your feet on the ground. If your toes are pointing out, it means that you are most likely clenching your buttocks.

Male ego is fragile and precious. Despite the fact that homosexuality is hugely accepted in our modern world, straight men still fear and resent any connotations that they might be gay. When I ask how they feel about anal stimulation, ninety percent respond that it feels wrong.

Much of the expectation to be masculine and straight comes from peer pressure. I have heard stories of young men being beaten up if they were not manly enough. This is a sad and scary reality.

Exercise:

I would like you to consider breaking this negative taboo in your life and getting an anal massage yourself. If you have done it before – wonderful! How was it? Would you do it again?

If this is a new idea for you, please give it a try. In all the anal massage sessions that I have ever given I only recall two cases where the men were too tense and reported discomfort. Everybody else had an amazing experience, often much to their own surprise.

You do not need to go as far as having internal stimulation. Just an external anal massage will be a great start. And you can ask your lover to do it for you; however, I would recommend a trained professional. I have actually heard of cases of painful or even traumatic anal experiences when performed by inexperienced partners.

PUTTING IT ALL TOGETHER

We have covered a lot of new ground in this section, and I hope that I have opened your mind to new possibilities of being receptive as a lover and of surrendering to your partner's touch.

I gave you a lot of guidance and practices that can help you open up to more pleasure and more wholeness in your sexuality and in your life. Remember, as long as you are denying or suppressing an aspect of your eroticism, something will be missing in your life. We are sexual beings by our very nature, and our bodies are beautiful and sensual in their wholeness, just as they are.

Despite all the negative messages we receive about sex, there is no denying that if there was no sex, there would be no life! In fact, sex is one of the most beautiful ways to express romantic love between partners. A woman's vagina is the gateway of all new life and as a man, you carry between your legs very sophisticated equipment that allows her to conceive that life in the first place.

We should stop demonizing sex and we should finally admit it – sex is wonderful and we love it!

So your homework includes scheduling and performing the following activities:

1/ Discussing with your partner four types of touch (Dr. Betty Martin's Wheel of Consent) and identifying which quadrants you both are in during different intimate activities.

Date: ....

2/ Allowing your partner to touch, tease and pleasure you while you simply surrender and receive. Make sure to start cultivating the attitude of complete and intense presence!

Date: ....

3/ Ask a partner/lover/friend/practitioner to assist you in a session of active receiving.

Date: ....

4/ Schedule an anal massage.

Date: ....

Part 5

NURTURING YOUR PARTNER

"When you are in love with a man or a woman, the love you feel does not come from him or her; it is the love flowing from your own heart that you feel. Your partner is simply giving you an excuse to love. Love is always found flowing in your heart, not in your family, lover, career or art."
— David Deida

HOMEMADE CHOCOLATE

To this day I cannot think of Aaron without a smile. He was a man with the physique of a cub and the spirit of a tiger. He had been teaching Tantra for many years, empowering people through workshops and one-on-one coaching to embrace sex as an integral and essential aspect of their lives. The first night we met he told me that we were going to have sex. He gave me his address and said that he was expecting me that evening. I said "forget it" and I made him wait a while. Three days to be exact.

When I arrived at his place, we did not talk much. He pinned me to the wall and fed me homemade chocolate, an aphrodisiac which he had prepared earlier on. This whole macho act was exciting at first, but quickly started to get old. I asked him to soften his approach and we finally sat down on his bed to chat.

I needed to connect with him first and I had questions. I needed to know what kind of expectations we both had about that evening. I needed to know his relationship status and whether some woman out there was going to hate me for being intimate with him. I needed to know his sexual health situation. And I needed him to be aware of my sexual journey. Well, a short version of it.

He answered all my questions patiently and then guided me through a tantric ritual creating a sacred space between us, consecrating our erotic energies and allowing us to relate to each other on a deeper level.

We did make love that night. And it was magical.

We made love on many more nights and each time he was guiding me deeper and deeper into my orgasmic self. He was a patient and generous lover, and he was an amazing teacher. He kept correcting my breathing, instructing my muscle control, helping me relax. I had full trust in his abilities as a lover and as a Tantra teacher, and I surrendered to his guidance and to his body completely.

And he made me orgasm – again and again, and again, in different ways, in different parts of my body, with different intensities. He even made me ejaculate. He showed my body what it meant to become so aroused that the orgasms just kept flowing through me, creating one long orgasmic state. My body shivered and buzzed under his touch. He was teaching me, he was healing me and he was awakening the goddess within me.

We were having a wonderful time, and we even occasionally left the bedroom.

What women want

In the previous section of this book you have received, you have surrendered and hopefully you had a wonderful time. Now you are going to give! But before you can truly give to your partner, you need to understand what it is that women want.

First of all, women want to surrender. As you will recall from previous chapters, surrender is deeply linked to the feminine nature and women yearn for it from their cores. In our lives we need to be in control of so many things, we need to be reasonable, accountable, we need to produce results, be on time and take care of others. In a state of deep surrender and raw passion, a woman can forget about all that and simply follow her untamed, authentic self. She can let go of all control and ride the waves of her arousal and her pleasure.

You can support her surrender by helping her to relax and feel safe. Relaxation is crucial for a woman to reach the heights of ecstasy. Tension, both physical and mental, will keep her from surrendering and from losing herself in ecstasy.

Safety refers to both external factors – like not having to worry that someone will walk in on you – and to the relationship between the two of you. She will feel safe with you if she can rely on you, if she knows that you will not abandon her, if she feels respected and seen by you. She will not feel safe if she is not certain whether she can trust you, if you had an argument earlier on that day or if she is feeling upset with you.

Second of all, women want you to be present; to truly show up as a man and a lover and to be fully there, fully connected, in the moment. If you are physically with her but at the back of your mind you are recalling the events from your day, if you are feeling upset about someone who annoyed you earlier on that day, if you are planning your to-do list for tomorrow or even if you are worrying about your erection and your performance as a lover, you are not present. To be present with her means to give her one hundred percent of your attention, to tune out the entire world and to commit to your experience with her – whether it lasts ten minutes or three hours. To hold her with the full intensity of your consciousness and your energy.

And thirdly, women want to connect emotionally; they want to connect through the heart. When you mix your loving energy with your erotic energy, you turn sex into lovemaking. And this applies whether you are being intimate with your wife, with a friend or with a stranger. In order to give her a deep and satisfying experience, you need to open your heart and hers.

You can do this simply by honestly sharing something with her, something that touched your heart – that made you feel an emotion. It can be any emotion – love, excitement, joy, gratitude, sadness, grief or longing. If the emotion has something to do with her, even better! Once you start talking, you will soon discover that she will most likely follow and open up her heart to you as well. This will create a beautiful depth and nurturing in your connection.

So what can you share with her? I will give you some examples.

"I love that smile that you always welcome me with when I come back home. You make me feel loved, cared for and deeply appreciated."

"I really enjoyed that walk we went for after dinner. I felt very connected to you as we were discussing our plans for next year. I love how much we both care about our relationship."

"Thank you so much for the beautiful dinner you made for us tonight. You nurture my body, my mind, my heart and my soul. And I love you."

"I felt worried and scared when I did not hear back from you the other day. I knew that you were driving and that you were tired. It was such a relief to finally hear from you and to know that you were safe. Thank you for reaching out as soon as you could."

In fact, you can use this technique outside the bedroom as well. You can use it over the dinner table, you can use it with your kids and entire family, you can use it with friends. You can create a theme; for example, everybody goes around the table and shares what they most love and appreciate about everybody else. Can you imagine the amazing experience of love, gratitude and appreciation that will fill the room?

The possible themes that you can explore with a lover are:

What you love about each other,

What you love about your life together,

What you are grateful for in your life,

What you enjoyed most lately,

What you worry about,

What you fear.

These themes will require you to become extremely open and authentic, even vulnerable. This can be challenging to many men. But I promise you that it is worth the effort.

When I work with couples and ask them to perform this exercise together, men are usually the ones who struggle with it a little more than the women. But once they do come up with five or so sentences, they feel extremely open, proud and happy. Many women feel so touched by this experience that they actually start to cry during this sharing time.

And then you will swap and you will witness her sharing. This can be a very humbling and eye opening experience. So be ready to have your heart opened and pierced to the core with the intensity of her true love and authentic passion. This might be an experience like nothing you have ever felt before!

KEYS TO HER KINGDOM

Aaron kept joking that a tantric 'quickie' would go on for at least an hour. As a lover, he could last forever and he had never ejaculated when we were together. That was his decision as I had never requested him to retain his semen during our intimate times. He was always choosing to sublimate his erotic energy, to move it up his body and to keep his sexual juices within. This can be easily and comfortably done when you are familiar with the practice of moving your arousal away from your genitals.

If you have played with the practices that I have been sharing with you throughout this book, you are at this stage aware of techniques and tools that you can use to spread your sexual energy through your body and to control your excitement. But I would not recommend abstaining from ejaculating completely until you are an experienced tantric lover. When clients ask me how often they should ejaculate, I always tell them to listen to their body. If your system is needing and asking for that release, allow it to happen and enjoy it. But also do make sure to experiment with semen retention for a few days or weeks. See how it feels – see what the fuss is all about!

Tantric men who practice ejaculatory choice do so because of the many benefits they obtain from it. They enjoy energizing, rejuvenating and nurturing their bodies with their life force, which they circulate daily throughout their system. This becomes easier and easier with practice, but typically you might need to spend about a year first training and preparing your body for a long term semen retention practice.

Another amazing outcome of this practice is mastering the separation of ejaculation and orgasm. When I say that tantric men do not ejaculate, I do not mean that they do not orgasm – quite the opposite, actually. Tantric men are multi-orgasmic and experience deep states of full-bodied pleasure and ecstasy.

Aaron and I shared many long moments of shared orgasmic bliss. We both kept coming again and again, at the same time or at different times. And the pleasure that was orgasmically exploding and expanding through his entire being left me without a doubt that a non-ejaculatory orgasm offers a depth of experience that is not possible during ejaculation. As Aaron's eyes were rolling backwards, his body shaking at his core, moved by the intensity of his orgasm, I was in pure awe of his masculine strength and discipline.

I have worked with so many men that I am fully aware of just how strong the attachment to ejaculation can be. And you do not need to give up that pleasure as the price of enjoying tantric delights. What I am encouraging you to do instead is to train your body to gain so much control that you can last as long as you want before ejaculating. That sounds fair enough, doesn't it?

And then if one day you decide to explore and experience the benefits of semen retention, you are free to do that too!

Tantric rituals

Aaron's deep insight into feminine pleasure and arousal allowed him to guide me to a level of ecstatic pleasure that I had not known before. And there is no way I can pass all his knowledge and experience on to you in this book, but I am going to give you a few keys in order to point you in the right direction.

Aaron recognized our bodies as sacred, as temples of pleasure and delight. He used his touch, his breath, his presence to honour and worship my body – and in particular my genitals. Tantra has beautiful Sanskrit words for our intimate parts. The female genitalia are called 'yoni', meaning 'sacred space' and man's penis is called 'lingam', meaning 'wand of light'.

This honouring, celebratory approach is the essence of Tantra. Tantra is not really a set of practices in the way the Kama Sutra is. Tantra is a philosophy, a mindset, a way to perceive your world and live your life. When you live tantrically, you recognize that every aspect of your life is sacred; you bring deep mindfulness into your everyday tasks and delight in life's little pleasures. When you make love tantrically, you perceive the divinity in your partner and in yourself, you treat your intimate time together as special, you celebrate it. You would not rush a Christmas dinner. Why would you rush sex?

Using tantric rituals is the simplest and most direct route to creating a sacred container of divine love and connection between the two of you.

Look deep into your partner and see a goddess within her – acknowledge that out loud. Look at her vulva and see it as a very special part of her body, worthy of respect and praise. In many ancient cultures the vulva was worshipped and cherished for being the source of life, the birthplace. Think of her vulva as a sacred garden – warm, moist, fertile and rich.

Sacred vulva

The vulva is very rich in nerve endings and hence very sensitive; she is an opening, full of pleasure, welcoming you in with anticipation, hunger and passion. Describe to your partner what her vulva looks like, the shape, colour, texture, smell. Tell her how gorgeous, magical and sweet she is and how much you enjoy worshipping and pleasuring her.

Many women have not seen other real vulvas and compare themselves to the airbrushed or surgically modified representations that we see in the media. The porn industry presents to us a very unified standard of female genitalia, but in reality all vulvas are different and unique.

Exercise:

Take your time to go on a tour of your woman's genitals. Explore her outer labia, notice their shape and colour. Observe the thickness or thinness of her skin, the amount of hair. Open her outer lips and have a good look at her inner lips. Examine her clitoris and the hood. Look for her urethral opening. Open her vagina. Use the sense of sight, touch, smell and taste. Get to know her yoni really well when not aroused and then repeat the same exercise in the state of arousal.

Keep describing to your partner what you are noticing.

Learn about her body

Did you know that your woman gets erections as well? Well, she does! Her genitals are full of erectile tissue that becomes engorged when she is aroused. All the blood rushing into her genitals will cause them to swell up and become darker in colour. Her genital engorgement will also cause her vagina to become tighter, which will in turn give you more intense sensations when you are inside her.

Get to know her erectile network. Familiarize yourself with female genital anatomy. Get a book on the subject or explore her body with your touch. Where is all the engorgeable tissue located? What muscles can you feel? What bones? How can you bring the most arousal and pleasure into her vulva? Use curiosity and playfulness, there is no right or wrong way to do it!

Magic of slowing down

In our fast-paced culture we are constantly rushing, multi-tasking, being as efficient as possible. Yet what your woman craves from you is to slow down. Do not take my word for it, test it! Tell her that next time you make love, you are going to make it a really slow experience. You will slow down your touch and you will really savour it. You will explore her body millimetre by millimetre looking for new sensations, waves of pleasure and vibration. You will make sure to connect with her deeply and take your time to arouse and tease her, creating an anticipation and hunger within her for your body and your penis. Ask her how she would feel about that and watch her eyes light up!

Slowing down will have another unexpected benefit for both of you; it will shift the dynamic in which she is always the gatekeeper of sex. In our society in general, men seek sex and women resist it. Men are so driven sexually and so in a rush to get into her pants that this often turns women off, and so you keep chasing while she is backing away.

The truth is that women are sexual beings as well and they do crave sex. The secret is to spark her desire so that instead of backing away, she is actively asking you for it. Your sexuality is valuable – it is a gift you can share with her instead of begging and pleading for it.

So instead of pushing for penetration with impatience, savour the foreplay. Relax into being playful, find pleasure in mutual touch, play with each moment. Start to seduce her, learn about her body and about all the ways that you can give her pleasure. Observe her reactions, tease and excite her. And then back away. Keep going towards her and then moving back. Allow her to start leaning towards you and observe how this new dynamic is blowing her mind.

Cherish her pearl

And above all, do not neglect her clitoris! This is the only body part known to man that was created solely for pleasure. The part you can touch and see at the top of her inner lips is her clitoral glans, and it contains a mind-blowing eight thousand nerve endings. This means that her pearl is very, very, very sensitive. As a comparison, the head of your penis contains about four thousand nerve endings on a much larger surface.

This extreme sensitivity is the reason why the clitoris is covered with a hood, to protect it from potentially painful friction with her underwear, hands, penis or other objects. This is why at the start you need to approach it with extreme caution and gentleness. And ideally with coconut oil. Fortunately, once she becomes more aroused, she can accept much more pressure and friction.

You might be surprised to learn that a woman's clitoris extends deep into her body. Behind the glans you will find the shaft of the clitoris which then connects to the clitoral legs, looking somewhat like a wishbone and enveloping the vaginal canal from both sides. The clitoris plays a very important function in a woman's arousal, and a skilful touch of her beloved will give her immense pleasure.

Aaron used a variety of ways to stimulate my clitoris and kept coming back to it regularly, each time giving my arousal a delicious boost. He played my body like an instrument and knew exactly which keys to push in order to get particular reactions from me.

How well do you know your partner's body?

ALL ABOUT THE BREASTS

Around the same time Aaron and I met, I was also exploring a connection with Josh. The two were complete opposites when it came to character and temperament. Quiet and withdrawn, Josh made me feel extremely safe and comfortable. I could just be my introverted self around him, while we chatted for hours, sharing our lives and our secrets with each other. He was cooking for me, he was listening to me and he was holding me in a warm, soft cloud of his loving attention.

He was a very slow and attentive lover. In fact, whenever I was with him, the whole world just seemed to slow down, luxuriously basking in each moment, relaxing in an awareness that there was absolutely nowhere else to be and nothing else to do.

He adored my body and I adored his touch. I particularly enjoyed the attention he gave my breasts. He loved to caress them with his hands, lips and tongue. And he was not in a rush either. He was either fully aware of just how much stimulation a female body needs in order to build up enough arousal, or he was indeed enjoying himself so much he did not want to move on. In either case, what he was doing was working great!

I still remember the first time he gave me a nipple-gasm. We were playing in his bed and he was really taking his time with my breasts. I was lying back and enjoying his touch. My body kept relaxing and opening up more and more to the pleasure he was giving me. I was letting out satisfied sounds and my body was gently undulating on the mattress.

My excitement was slowly building up as I felt strong, electric energy shooting down from my breasts to my genitals. I was absolutely loving the pleasure he was giving me; the stimulation was absolutely perfect. His touch was not too firm and not too light. I could feel myself getting wet while delicious heat was spreading through my vagina. I did not want him to stop!

And then it happened! The erotic charge in my breasts exploded through my chest as the pleasure was almost too much to handle. A warm wave of a loving energy kept expanding through my system, starting in my heart and then rippling out through my body. I was mind-blown, I was in a trance, I was floating in a deeply orgasmic state as my whole body was trembling in ecstasy.

When I was finally able to control my muscles, I reached out and held Josh tight, his chest firmly pressed against mine, both of us swimming in the golden glow of my nipple-gasm.

Energetic polarity

In my experience, as much as men love breasts, they rarely ever spend too much time on them. Some fondling, followed by a few kisses and then men are off to the genitals. But there is a very important reason to give your partner's chest a lot more attention.

Tantra describes a polarity that exists between lovers and within our bodies themselves. We are all like magnets in a way; we have two magnetic poles that the energy flows between. One pole is the active one that the energy flows from (called the north pole), and the other pole is receptive because the energy flows towards it (the south pole).

For a person with a male body, the active pole is located in the genitals, and the receptive pole is in the chest. For a person with a female body, this polarity is reversed. This dynamic explains why men are usually so sex driven while women are more focused on feeling love. Have you ever wondered why so often you need to jump through hoops in order to have sex with a woman? Why you need to take her out, buy her flowers and create an emotional connection between the two of you? This is why – her active pole is in her heart and it needs to become activated first. You need to open her heart before you can open her legs.

This is also why men do not need as much wining and dining and actually often need to sleep with a woman first, before they know if they love her.

When lovers get together, the erotic energy starts to flow between their bodies in a circle. From the man's active pole, his penis, into his lover's receptive pole, her vagina and then up to her heart and from there, from her active pole, into his receptive pole – his heart. From his heart the energy will naturally cycle back down into his penis, and so on. This circle of sexual energy feels absolutely exquisite, particularly when lovers have a strong polarity between them, which is not always the case. People who are naturally sensitive to energy will be able to detect and experience this flow fairly strongly, but everybody else can learn to feel it as well.

Exercise:

Try this exercise with a lover: sit down on the floor or a bed and face each other. Bring your pelvises close together by spreading your legs out. Your lover's legs can rest on top of yours. You can hold hands or allow them to rest on each other's hips or legs. Look into each other's eyes and synchronize your breathing so that you are inhaling together and exhaling together. Next, visualize the circle of energy flowing between your bodies, starting in your penis and then flowing to her vagina, up her body and out of her heart into yours. Use your breath to support this visualization, and imagine sending the energy out to her as you exhale and receiving it into your heart as you inhale. You can also try this exercise with alternating breath – she will be inhaling as you are exhaling and vice versa – if you want to make sure you are both visualizing the same movement at the same time.

And now just relax and stay there. Let go of any thoughts, do not analyse this experience, let go of any mind chatter. Keep bringing your attention back to your body if you become distracted and feel into the experience you are having. What can you feel in your body? How is your system responding to this practice? Are you enjoying it? What can you sense energetically?

You can do this for one minute, for five minutes or for half an hour. It is completely up to you, but try not to rush it. Take your time to fully drop into this experience. You can try closing your eyes if it allows you to stay more present.

Breasts and arousal

As you are now aware, a woman's north pole – her heart – is very important in her decision whether to sleep with you or not. But it is also very important when it comes to her arousal response itself.

For men arousal is usually fairly easy because their active pole is in their penis. It is, however, a very different story for a woman. She needs her active pole, her chest, to be awakened first.

Women can still become aroused through genital touch alone and often do when they try to have sex like a man. But when accessed through her breasts, her arousal will be much richer, it will have a completely different depth, a different quality to it and it will flow easier through her entire body. It will also bring much more nurturing and satisfaction into her sex as opposed to a genitally focused experience which, in the long term, will make her feel depleted and frustrated.

Exercise:

Next time you are with your lover, make sure to spend much more time with her breasts than you usually do. Remember not to go for her nipples too quickly; they are very sensitive and will become much more ready for touch once she is aroused. Caress, massage and lick her breasts while checking in with her about the pressure and speed of the stimulation. Many men use way too much pressure on the breasts, which can actually turn her off. Women usually complain that their partners do not know how to touch their breasts, so keep seeking feedback.

Experiment with different kinds of touch and strokes. Be curious, ask her what she enjoys the most and how she touches her breasts herself. Learn about her breasts and about how they respond to stimulation. I promise that you will make your lover one extremely happy and satisfied woman!

TANTRIC MASSAGE

I used to think that orgasm was a pleasurable experience centred in my genitals, accompanied by pulsations of the pelvic floor muscle, and that the whole thing lasted a few seconds. I was wrong.

Or to be more accurate, I only knew a tiny aspect of the story.

Orgasm is defined in Tantra as a release or movement of energy through one's system. And it can happen both with those pelvic spasms and without them. The energy can flow in one potent outburst or it can keep flowing in waves for hours. It can be centred in the genitals or can have absolutely nothing to do with them. It can be accompanied by a strong emotion or not. You might feel like uncontrollably laughing out loud. Or like sobbing in despair.

I do have mixed feelings about many people working in the tantric industry, and I always do my due diligence research when it comes to judging someone's ability and skill. So when Shantam Nityama came to town, I knew everything about him that I could have possibly learned through online research and seeking the opinions of others. I was excited to attend his weekend workshop and I booked an individual session with him a few days later. He was making huge promises and I was ready to find out more about him and his method for myself.

During the workshop I was mind-blown by the depth of his wisdom and experience. And by his arrogance.

I made a lot of notes that weekend and started to look forward to my one-on-one experience with him. Nityama created a method of bodywork called 'Nitvana' where he facilitates full body orgasmic states and emotional healings for his clients. He became particularly known in the world for taking people through these deep experiences without using any touch. I knew in theory what he was doing during these sessions, but I was keen to find out in practice how he worked.

When I arrived for my session, he was still having his breakfast and was in no hurry to finish it. We started chatting as I was discreetly watching the clock. At $1200 for a two hour session, this was the most expensive breakfast meeting I had ever attended.

Next he moved on to reading my Human Design chart and it was at least another hour before I finally made it onto the massage table. Fortunately, Nityama did deliver generously in the end as the session went on for six hours instead of two!

He kept guiding me with his voice and with his hands. He took me into a deeply orgasmic state and he kept me there for hours. He started by guiding me to build up a high level of energy with my breath. He was not massaging my body but he was holding different points, directing the energy flow through my system. So he did use touch after all, but I did not mind; I still learned from him everything that I wanted to learn.

Creating a tantric experience

One of the most beautiful gifts you can give to your lover is a gift of a sensual massage. As she relaxes completely, gently guided by your touch and voice, there is nothing she needs to do – just let go and receive. And you do not need to have a degree in massage therapy either in order to give her a wonderful experience! Giving each other a sensual massage is way easier than you think.

In fact during an experience of erotic massage, you are able to take her into a higher ecstatic peak than most women experience during intercourse. So it is definitely worth playing with.

A tantric massage is a form of a sensual massage that consists of three steps. First you are going to connect with her, next you are going to relax her and then finally you are going to arouse her.

For the connecting part, start by inviting your partner to sit down facing you, close her eyes and take a few deep breaths. You can even meditate together for a few minutes. Letting go of the busyness of the day will be very helpful for a deeper experience. You do not really want her to be stuck in her head thinking about that unpleasant person she met in the supermarket or the bills she will need to pay later.

When both of you open your eyes again, begin with five minutes of eye-gazing. All you need to do is to look into each other's eyes without speaking. Giggles might happen as a natural response to feeling awkward. Simply acknowledge them with a smile and go back to being silent. Eye contact is a very intimate experience, as our eyes are windows to the soul. This is why a prolonged eye contact feels so challenging for most people. Do not let it discourage you and give it a go. Eye-gazing can actually induce a state of mild trance and turn into a deeply spiritual experience of seeing into each other like you have never before.

After you have finished, share your experience with each other.

Next, open your hearts and connect with each other emotionally. Express a few things about your emotional state and about your connection with your lover in the way that you learned at the beginning of this part of the book. Enjoy this process and do not take yourself too seriously. You are creating a beautiful tantric experience for your beloved, and as much as possible it should be a playful one.

Now is the time to create a circle of energy between your bodies, so feel free to bring your pelvises together and to synchronize your breathing while you visualize your energy circling between the two of you. Try to do this for at least five minutes as well. Let go of any expectations; simply experience and explore.

At this stage both of you should feel fairly connected, and so it is time to invite your woman to lie down on her front and to start relaxing her body. If you know any massage strokes, feel free to use them. Otherwise, start by gently stroking her entire body with some soft fabric – you can use a tassel, a soft feather, a sarong or maybe a piece of velvet. Try different textures and see what works best for her.

When using your fingers, start by caressing her skin with featherlight strokes. Take your time and keep gliding over her entire body from head to toe. You can then apply more pressure, still using your hands. Applying oil to her skin might be helpful now. You can also use firmer pressure while pushing down on her body and holding still for a moment, working your way from her feet all the way up to her shoulders and down her arms. Imagine that you are making love to her skin with your hands.

Take your time. After about fifteen minutes of this massage, she will start to melt under your touch. At that stage, ask her to turn over and repeat this relaxing process on her front. Avoid her breasts and her genitals for the moment.

After you have completed step two, you can move on to step three. As you are well aware now, her energy flows abundantly from her chest, so start by giving her a loving breast massage. Keep asking for feedback until you are satisfied that she is truly enjoying your touch. Use massaging oil and play with different strokes; allow your imagination to guide you. Again, there are no wrong or right ways to do it. The fun is in exploring and learning what works best for her.

Ask whether she is ready for genital touch and if she confirms that she is, place your hand over her yoni. Do not do anything, just hold her. Allow her to relax under your hand and remind her to keep breathing deeply. Whenever you notice that she is holding her breath, guide her to relax and let go of any tension.

If it is more comfortable for you, you can sit down between her legs and start to gently massage her vulva. Do not go straight for the clitoris; play with her entire erectile network and keep arousing her through your teasing. Massage her inner thighs, her groin creases, her pubic bone. Caress her outer lips, her inner lips, her vaginal opening. Once you notice that she is getting wet – and particularly if she has begged you enough for it – play with her clit. But when you do, keep erring on the side of caution – her pearl is very, very, very sensitive!

If she is open to it, move your touch inside of her vagina, but do make sure to ask first. Once inside, you can apply the mapping process or just keep caressing her G-spot, her vaginal walls and her cervix if you can reach it. Do not try to make her come. If she does orgasm, wonderful! But do not make this experience about climax. Tantric massage is about guiding her into a deep state of pleasure and erotic embodiment without placing any requirements on her.

Many women feel pressured to orgasm when their partner is touching their clit. But this mental tension only inhibits their ability to climax. So make sure that she is relaxed and open. Let her know that there is no goal here. That you simply want her to feel pleasure and to connect to her sensuality.

After the session comes to a natural end, give her a few minutes of silent integration. Stay next to her and hold space for her experience. Do not rush off anywhere in case she needs anything.

Do not require her to return the favour that same evening. She will most likely be in a state of deep, erotic trance. Allow her to stay there as long as she wishes to and cater for any needs she might have. She might want water or a hug. Or she might want to make love. Allow her to decide.

ANAL PLAY FOR WOMEN

Before I discovered Tantra, my experiences of anal sex were few and far between. And for a good reason! My pre-Tantra lovers really did not know how to approach my anus properly and so they were causing me more pain than pleasure. And frankly, there really was not that much pleasure there, if any at all. So I kept avoiding anal sex, only agreeing to it if my lover really insisted. In some cases, we actually were not able to go ahead with it as it was just too painful for me.

Fast forward a few years and things have changed a lot! I do need to thank the Institute of Somatic Sexology for this in a huge way. My experience with them was very unique and different from other trainings I had attended. Over a period of six months, I had to complete assignments that required me to work on the bodies of willing friends and lovers. I also had to perform the same tasks on my own body, plus I had other students work on me while I was doing the same for them. It was a profound journey of deep healing for myself as well as others.

To witness others undergoing a deep and meaningful process under the touch of my hands was humbling and extremely valuable for my experience. To also have same experiences for myself – to feel the amazing healing power of skilful touch combined with the loving presence of a competent practitioner – made it all even more real and enriching.

I think all of us students were a little anxious about the anal module. I had plenty of experience giving anal touch, but receiving it was a different matter altogether! For the first assignment, I had to give an anal massage to myself – both external and internal. I actually had to approach this exercise twice. The first time I felt absolutely no sensations in my anus. I could feel the pressure of my fingers on and around my anus but the experience was absolutely neutral – no pleasure, no pain, no arousal, no discomfort – just numbness. I was so confused that I discontinued the session and decided to try again on another day.

During the second approach, I started to experience pleasure during the external massage. I understood that I must have carried a lot of shame around my anus, which led to dissociating from that area completely. Many people experience numbness in their genitals and anuses due to years of carrying chronic tension there or pushing these intimate body parts out of their consciousness due to ongoing feelings of shame, embarrassment or trauma.

I figured that my anus had started to open up a bit to sensations after my first try. As I kept stroking it externally, I could feel different degrees of pleasure. And all was well until I started applying gentle pressure on the anus itself to see if it would invite some internal touch. As I was gently pushing my finger in as much as my relaxed anus would allow, I suddenly noticed fear and anxiety in my body. The possibility of being penetrated there really scared me. I calmed myself down and reassured myself that I would only go as far as my anus would allow. I thought about all the times that men forced their penises inside my anus without sufficient preparation and lubrication, causing me pain and feelings of being violated and abused.

It took me another little while before my body was able to start allowing internal touch. Either from myself or from others.

Fortunately, perseverance and patience do pay off as now I am comfortably able to include anal play in my sex life. I recognize my anus as a source of pleasure, as an erotic part of my body, and I am having an increasingly loving relationship with it. Gentle touch and breathing exercises do wonders when it comes to healing dissociation and trauma in the body. And since there are hardly any people out there who are free of any anal trauma or shame, this area should always be treated with the utmost kindness and loving care.

The rules of anal sex

As well as men, women are also capable of experiencing intense pleasure in their anuses. However, in order to have a truly enjoyable experience, you need to be aware of the rules of anal sex.

Dr. Jack Morin was an American pioneer in the field of anal pleasure, and over many years he had done a lot of marvellous work helping men and women reclaim erotic pleasure in their anuses and to heal the phenomenon of "genital hole" – a high degree of dissociation and numbness many people experience there. I learned a lot from him about anal touch and if you are interested in delving into this subject much deeper, you should definitely research his work.

Here is what you need to know in order to be successful in your anal play:

1/ Anal touch should never, ever hurt. If it does – you are doing it wrong. Anal sphincters are muscle rings located at the entrance of the anus which are meant to keep things moving out. If something is introduced from the outside (a finger, penis or a toy), these muscles will tense up in order to stop the intrusion. Instead of forcing items in, you need to massage the anus externally first, in order to relax the sphincters before the insertion.

2/ There is no natural lubrication in the anus so you always need to use a lubricant during anal play. As usual, I recommend coconut oil.

3/ Past the anal sphincters, you will encounter the rectum. Faeces are not normally stored in there until just before the bowel movement. You can, however, encounter traces of faeces in there. If that is a problem for either of you, I recommend having an enema.

4/ For most couples, anal sex does not include using the penis. Instead, they prefer using fingers or toys. Oral stimulation of the anus is called rimming and can be a source of a lot of pleasure. Using vibrating toys externally or internally can add an exciting level of pleasure.

5/ There are health risks associated with anal contact and if you are worried about STI's, make sure to use a barrier – a condom for insertion or a dental dam for rimming.

6/ Keep communicating during the experience. The person being penetrated always has the final say when it comes to the anal stimulation. Nothing should be inserted into the anus until the recipient of the touch is ready and keen. As soon as they say 'stop', this should be fully respected. The anus is a highly sensitive area and as such, it can be both a source of a lot of pleasure and a lot of pain. As soon as the pleasure turns into pain, all touch should be stopped.

7/ Many men enjoy prostate stimulation. The prostate is located on the belly side of the rectum, about two knuckles in.

8/ It is possible to experience anal orgasms, even without any direct genital stimulation. In my experience, this is not very common but it does happen sometimes; particularly when the person being anally stimulated is not determined to have an orgasm, but rather is completely immersed in the moment and in the pleasure they are experiencing, without any goals or expectations.

9/ If you are using toys, make sure to pick the ones with a flared base as it is possible to lose items inside the anus.

10/ Due to a sedentary lifestyle, trauma or shame, many people hold chronic tension inside the anus which can make insertion difficult and uncomfortable. In such cases, I recommend gently inserting the tip of your own finger into the anus while in the shower or a bath and trying to consciously relax the anal sphincters. When done on a regular basis, this practice will allow you to enjoy anal stimulation much more.

If you are still feeling a bit uncertain about anal stimulation, I would recommend using nitrile gloves. This can provide a level of comfort to both parties from the hygiene perspective, and also for the protection of the receiver as nails or hard skin can feel unpleasant against the soft tissue of the anal canal.

As long as you are keeping in mind the rules of anal sex, you are very likely to give your beloved a very beautiful, safe and even ecstatic experience of anal pleasure.

Above all, take your time, stay curious, keep checking in with her and use plenty of lubrication. You might even discover that your partner becomes open to the idea of anal intercourse if this is something she had been opposed to before.

PLEASURE MAP

A wonderful and fun practice for couples is to create a pleasure map of your partner's body. This is a practice created by another one of my wonderful teachers – Kenneth Ray Stubbs. Many of us feel awkward and shy about discussing our sexual preferences, even with our partners. So as they attempt to give us pleasure in ways that have worked for their previous lovers, we might end up enduring and tolerating their touch rather than blissfully enjoying it.

I first experienced the process of pleasure mapping during a one day workshop conducted by Deej Juventin and Uma Furman from the Institute of Somatic Sexology. All participants were divided into pairs and we were practicing on each other. First my partner was mapping my body and then I got to map his. The second part of the exercise particularly blew my mind as I learnt how easy it can be to find out exactly how to give your partner the most pleasure. This takes all the guessing out of the equation and allows you to give your beloved a wonderful touch with pure confidence that they are loving every moment of it.

Exercise:

Lovers can perform this exercise naked or partly naked if they wish. Ask your partner to lie down comfortably while you are going to turn into a 'pleasure researcher'. You are going to start touching different areas of her body, while she will give you feedback each time. Her feedback will be a number ranging from minus three to plus three. Zero is neutral, plus three is fantastic, minus three indicates discomfort, and the remaining numbers advise about different degrees of desirability in between the extremes.

Try different kinds of touch on each area ranging from a soft caress to a firm pressure. You can also play with gentle slapping, light scratching, kisses, licking, or using your feet, feathers, fabrics, oils, lotions or vibrators. Remember that you are looking for pleasure, so do not stay for too long anywhere where she indicates any minus number. Unless your partner enjoys pain, in which case you can do more of a pain mapping using biting, hard slapping or clothespins.

The smaller the areas you are mapping, the more precise information you will gather. You can also perform micro-mapping where you are going to explore in detail just one part of her body.

This exercise should be performed on a regular basis in order to fully explore and create each other's pleasure map. Many people can spend many years together without a clear understanding of their partner's favourite erogenous zones and their full pleasure potential. So even if you do feel confident about your familiarity with her body, this technique will reveal new things to you. Be ready to be surprised!

Challenges of a long-term connection

The majority of people that seek my advice tell me about their frustrations with their routine and boring sex lives. As most of us usually lack any in-depth sexual education, many couples resort to the same sexual activities over many years. And regardless how exciting these activities once were, when repeated on end, they will eventually start to bore us.

This is where introducing pleasure mapping – plus many of the other sexual games described in this book – is a fantastic way to keep the excitement alive and sex enticing.

Another problem worth mentioning is a growing problem of older men developing erectile difficulties. As producing an erection becomes a challenge, many couples assume that it must put an end to their sexual activity together. But that does not need to be the case. First of all, erectile dysfunction can be treated successfully and on top of that, as I have just pointed out, there are many ways to play together that do not require a hard penis. Even penetration is possible without an erection when your partner is on top. Ask her to use lubrication and to gradually feed your penis inside of her vagina using her fingers. Next, instead of using the standard up and down movement, she can move her hips in gentle circles, allowing your penis to stimulate her and yourself at the same time.

Where there is a will, there is a way!

Do not allow your relationship to become another sexless marriage; there are already too many of these around. Use curiosity, creativity and maybe even some expert advice in order to keep cultivating your intimate connection over any length of time you get to spend together.

Nurture your passion, entice her desire and keep playing, exploring, enjoying. There is no limit to the depth of intimacy that you can reach together!

CRAZY, SEXY LOVE

There is no way I can conclude this part without telling you about Chris. What he gave me as a man and as a lover was completely not what I expected. But it was something I desperately needed.

When I first met him, I had been involved exclusively with tantric lovers and I was not looking for anybody from outside of that circle. I did not want to come back to 'normal sex', nor did I want to have any sexual experiences that were not tantric.

We met at a dance event and had a playful time together before even exchanging names or speaking a word to each other. Handsome and a great dancer, Chris soon turned out to be very smart and funny too. He asked me out and we had a wonderful time together. The second time we met, he invited me over to his place for dinner and I found myself very conflicted about our catch up. Not long before that, I had been shamed for sleeping with men too quickly and I was trying to get to the bottom of that. I sat with that for a while; I spoke to my friends about it, even sought professional advice. But the conclusion from all directions was that pretending to be a prude was not real to me, and would not serve me or those around me.

Still a little confused, I turned up at Chris' doorstep. I decided to enjoy myself, but without taking things to the bedroom. I wanted to experiment with this prudish approach and see how it felt to me.

We chatted, we ate and we drank wine. He was easy to talk to and fun company. At one point, he grabbed my hand and pulled me to the couch. We kept chatting there but not for much longer before his lips found mine. He was very strong, overpowering. I did not seem to have any say in our sensual exchange, but I felt very comfortable with that. He started to remove my clothes and I suddenly saw a bright red light bulb inside of my head – this would lead to sex!

Still, I remained completely unable to object as things were getting really steamy between us. Half clothed, he effortlessly picked me up, my legs wrapped around his waist, and he started carrying me to his bedroom. A faint voice in my head kept saying 'no' while my body was screaming one big, ecstatic 'yes!'. We did not even make it to the bedroom when he pinned me to the wall and our hot and horny fun continued there. At that point I started to orgasm.

Horny Chris was a force of nature to be reckoned with. Being in his arms felt like being in the middle of a wild storm – there is no way I was actually capable of doing anything except for trying to hold on to anything I could.

A creative and confident lover, he was taking my body on a wild ride. This was not tantric sex, this was fucking. It was raw, pure, animalistic sex. And I loved it!

A few times he pushed my body too hard, but he backed off every time I asked him to. Behind his brute strength there was a loving care and gentleness. I felt perfectly safe and relaxed in his embrace.

When we finally made it to his bed and slowly lost the rest of our clothes, the penetrative sex was just as wild and raw. There is no way I could tell you how many times I orgasmed. It felt like each orgasm kept flowing from the previous one, placing me in a complete whirlwind of orgasmic bliss and oblivion. His body was so strong, so masculine ... It was so easy to surrender to him, to let go and to flow with that crazy river of stimulation and excitement.

When he finally came, we collapsed into each other, breathless and ecstatic.

I could not help but wonder – why have I never experienced sex like this before? With all my previous experience, no one ever just took me, claimed me as his and fucked me breathless like this. We chatted about that while he was holding my naked body next to his.

And that faint voice of reason in my head? It was gone and has never come back!

Polarized couples

Do you remember the first thing that women really want, from the beginning of this part?

Surrender!

The more feminine the woman is, the more she will want to surrender. The more masculine the man is, the more he will want to dominate her. I kept telling Chris that he was an exquisite lover. He kept replying that it was me who was the wild one. The truth is that we had an extremely strong polarity between us.

Most people have a good feel about where they find themselves on the scale going from the extremely masculine, through neutral, all the way to the extremely feminine. There are very masculine men, there are more neutral, balanced men and there are feminine men. There are women who are fairly masculine, neutral or extremely feminine. As David Deida explains in his book *The way of the superior man*:

"You are always attracted to your sexual reciprocal. So, if you have a more feminine sexual essence, you will be attracted to a more masculine woman. You have probably seen men and women in couples like this. The man is more radiant and lively than the woman. The woman is more committed to her direction in life than the man. The relationship is more important to the man, whereas the woman likes to be left alone much of the time. These are signs of a relationship where the man has a more feminine essence and the woman's essence is more masculine.

"Other men, with more neutral sexual essences, prefer women who are also more neutral, neither particularly masculine nor feminine. This kind of couple can talk about anything, and they like talking about everything. They share hobbies, friends, even career goals. Though equally loving, this kind of couple is usually less sexually passionate than highly polarized couples. It would be unusual to hear about this kind of neutral or balanced couple yelling at each other, throwing pillows, wrestling each other down to the floor, and passionately making love right there and then."[11]

Chris is one of the more masculine men I know, while I am very feminine. The combination of our highly polarized sexual energies kept creating a wild storm every time we got together.

There are a lot of masculine men out there; in fact, the majority of men are masculine while the majority of women are feminine. The difference between Chris and my other masculine lovers was that he was not afraid to take me, to throw me on the bed, to rip my clothes off and have his way with me in any place or position that he fancied. At the same time he knew that I had my own voice and would tell him in no uncertain terms if I was not happy with what he was doing. This mutual understanding created safety and respect. And within that boundary of consent, we were free to play and enjoy.

So what did Chris give me, really? He met my need to surrender. And he gave me a gift of his masculine presence, strength and will. These are masculine qualities which women find very attractive.

I guess what I want you to take out of this chapter is that along with all the slowing down, connecting, creating a deep intimacy and love in your relationship, there is also room for raw, animalistic passion and uninhibited, authentic, wild sex. If that is something you both agree to!

PUTTING IT ALL TOGETHER

I hope that you have already used some of the techniques described in this part of the book. But if not, here is a short summary and a gentle encouragement to give these practices a go!

1/ Practice giving her what she wants:
   a. Help her relax and surrender
   b. Show up for her in your full masculine presence
   c. Connect with her through your heart

2/ Get to really know her body and her desire:
   a. Train your body and learn to ride the waves of arousal so that you can penetrate her for as long as she needs,
   b. Celebrate your intimate time together, honour her body with your touch, kisses and caresses, acknowledge the goddess within her,
   c. Get to know her sacred garden, study her vulva when not aroused and when aroused, explore her genital anatomy

and her erectile network,

d. Slooooooow dooooooown! Savour the touch, explore her entire body, connect with her deeply, keep extending the pleasure, arousing her, enticing her desire, teasing her ...

e. Keep coming back to her clitoris whenever you want to give her arousal a boost.

3/ Take care of her breasts before you touch her genitals. Learn how she likes them massaged, caressed, kissed, licked and stimulated. Do not forget that her energy flows from her chest!

4/ Give her a tantric massage. Schedule this with her and then take her luxuriously through the three steps – connecting, relaxing and finally, arousing. Do not rush the process; allow her to sink deep into a blissful state of orgasmic pleasure.

5/ Discuss anal play with her and see if she is open to some fun and exploration, keeping in mind the rules of anal sex.

6/ Create a pleasure map of her body. Do it regularly, do it often. Keep studying her body. This is not an activity you should do only once!

7/ Explore your animalistic side and see if you can include it in your sex life. Discuss it with her to make sure no boundaries are crossed!

Part 6
DISCOVERING YOUR FULL ORGASMIC POTENTIAL

"Most things in the world are hyped. Most things
are over-sold and under-delivered, but in my
experience sex, music, and psychedelics deliver.
They are actually better than advertised."
— Terence McKenna

ENTRANCED AND BREATHLESS

I feel so blessed for having met so many special, unique and beautiful men on my tantric path. Mostly through different workshops and events, I have had the pleasure and delight of spending time with and getting to know some truly amazing, smart, vulnerable, authentic, passionate and open-minded human beings that I have been able to talk with, cry with and even make love to if it felt right.

Jeremy was one of them. Shy in his own confident way, he did not speak very often but when he did, everybody listened. We met during a weekend workshop, and quite accidentally we ended up having lunch together. I did not take much notice of him at the beginning of the workshop, but by the time we were finished eating, I knew that I would see him again.

A few days later I invited him over and we had a lovely time, chatting, eating, laughing and making love. He was an amazing lover – very tantric, strongly multi-orgasmic, very connected to his body and very responsive to mine. Making love to him felt like dancing – fun, effortless, flowing.

After another few days, he asked me to come over to his place for dinner. Eating home-cooked meals with friends is one of my favourite things to do, whether I am the one cooking or whether somebody else is cooking for me. Plus, I was ready for more of his loving and his orgasmic touch.

We lived quite far away from each other so as I got into my car, preparing for an hour-long drive, I wondered how I should best spend that time. Apart from driving the car, of course.

I decided to build up my sexual energy and to play with my arousal. I started with some genital breathing, bringing a lot of awareness and relaxation into my yoni. She felt keen, open and hot. I was sending her my loving attention, feeling into her wetness and warmth.

Then I remembered the way one of my lovers used to kiss my breasts. His lips would wander all over my breast and even off of it, teasing me mercilessly, until he would finally place them around my nipple and suck it gently. He was sending me absolutely crazy with desire and passion. I would have done anything as long as he did not stop! My body will never forget the way his lips and tongue felt on my skin.

It was easy to start fantasizing about him, sucking and licking my breasts again. First the right one, taking his time, slowly, gently, patiently … And then the left one …

I must have spent at least half an hour during my trip imagining him pleasuring me. The drive was easy, mostly on a freeway. My eyes fixed on the road, my mind kept taking me into a deeper and deeper state of pleasure, passion and sensual bliss.

By the time I got to Jeremy's place, my cheeks were pink, my body blissfully relaxed and my yoni dripping wet. I did not tell him about any of that.

He hugged me and invited me in. As we kept chatting, he prepared dinner and dessert. His Greek background and his love for great food were a great combination and led to a deliciously decadent meal.

My sexual energy was slowly settling down, and I felt pretty calm by the time he took me to his bedroom. Fully clothed, I lay down on his bed, on my stomach, having a curious look around as he went to the bathroom. When he came back, he covered my body with his and started sensually thrusting his pelvis into mine, from behind. From the very first thrust, my erotic energy shot straight through me, from my pelvis all the way up to my head. I was immediately mind-blown and aroused beyond belief! As he kept thrusting, I almost came, still fully dressed.

God, there is such a delicious quality to making love through your clothes ... Like teenagers, enjoying the forbidden delights of a new sexual connection ...

When Jeremy finally turned me over, I was in a blissful trance, completely immersed in my senses and delights of my body.

We removed our clothes and played with each other's bodies for a while. I was loving his strong masculine physique! Kissing and caressing his chest, belly and thighs, I was loving his skin, enjoying his arousal.

When he finally entered me, I was lying on my back, on top of his body, as he was penetrating me from behind. It is quite an unusual position for me and I cannot even remember how our bodies ended up there. All I can remember is that his penis finally entering my vagina felt so incredibly good! I was gasping in ecstasy and within seconds I reached the most intense full-body orgasm I had ever had with a partner!

I was screaming in pleasure more intense than I could handle. I could not have cared less about Jeremy's housemates downstairs. They did not exist. All that existed was the bedroom and me, and Jeremy, and my orgasm, so deep and profound there are no words that could ever describe it. It kept going and going, and going, in ecstatic waves of pleasure expanding deliciously through my entire body and way past it, beyond my being, out into the Universe.

When I finally became quiet, I rolled off of Jeremy's body and he held me close. My body, shivering gently, felt good in his embrace.

When I was finally able to speak, we spoke softly about our experience.

And then we kept going. After another hour and a half of love-making, we finally fell asleep.

For both of us, this was the best and most intense sexual experience to date!

Preparation is key!

Having great sex does not come naturally to most people. It usually takes skill, patience, education and preparation. In the same way we invest in our professional skills or in our hobbies, we should also invest time and effort in our lovemaking abilities.

I lost count a long time ago of books I read, videos I watched, hours of practice I had done, workshops I attended, trainings and research I had done, deep conversations I had had with clients, friends, mentors and teachers in the sex and Tantra industry. And I am definitely not saying that you need to neglect your life and throw yourself into a pursuit of knowledge about good sex. I have a passion for great sex and will go to any length to learn all I can about it and to become the best sexuality coach and lover I can possibly be.

All I am saying is that if you want certain results, you need to put some work in.

As Einstein once pointed out, you cannot expect different results if you keep doing the same things. So I challenge you here to figure out what kind of a lover you want to be and what kind of sex you want to have – both solo sex and partner sex.

And then take steps to get there. Schedule a session with a practitioner, attend a workshop, read a book, do some research ... Anything will be better than nothing, particularly if you add practice to your explorations (sexplorations).

I put into practice pretty much everything I learn about, particularly when it comes to sex. I do not take anybody's word for it; I test it for myself and if it serves me, I will use it in my life. Or adapt it so it suits me better. Or discard it if it is not for me at that particular time.

So what kind of sex do you want to have?

And how can you prepare for it?

MEETING GOD THROUGH ORGASM

I had spent countless hours playing with edging. It is one of my favourite techniques, and it never fails to produce results. If you build up your level of arousal and sexual energy high enough and if you fill your entire body with that erotic charge, it will always lead to an intense and expansive orgasm.

As I keep taking myself almost to the edge of coming and then stop the stimulation and take deep, full breaths, my pleasure and arousal keep spilling out of my genitals and circulating all over my relaxed body. I can keep going like this for an hour or more, but even a half hour practice will produce yummy results.

In many cases, before I even take myself into that final orgasmic peak, I will experience trance-like states of deep ecstatic bliss. And it still consistently blows my mind just how much pleasure my body is capable of producing and experiencing.

I absolutely love this game where the desire for orgasm becomes so strong that taking away sexual stimulation feels almost torturous.

But I know that it is always worth it and I keep going, sinking deeper and deeper into my ecstatic state. My brain actually starts rewarding me with orgasmic responses before I even reach orgasm, and that feels freaking awesome as I keep extending these sensations over an hour or longer instead of having one short orgasmic peak!

I still remember one particular time in my early explorations, when I had my first ever spiritual experience during orgasm. I was lying in my bed, really taking my time. I started by caressing my entire body while keeping my breath deep and steady. When I started stroking my vulva and stimulating my vaginal canal, I knew I was in no hurry whatsoever to finish. I kept using my breath to spread the delicious sensations until my entire body felt like an ocean of sensual bliss and erotic pleasure.

As I finally orgasmed, my body became weightless and, in fact, did not feel physical anymore. I could not even sense the mattress underneath me. All I could feel was vibrating energy of intense pleasure spreading out through my entire being and out into the Universe. I could not tell where my body ended or began. I was limitless, I was energy, ever expanding, connected with every being and place on the planet and way beyond it.

I was expansive, I was ecstatic, I was everywhere. I was God.

Anatomy of arousal

This trance-like state is a result of both the body and brain working together. The brain acts as a pleasure centre, and the body keeps sending information to the brain through different sets of nerves located in the areas being stimulated. The glans of a woman's clitoris is extremely sensitive and contains around 8,000 nerve endings. Her entire vulva (external genitalia) is very nerve rich and there are also nerve endings inside her vagina; however, not as many and most of them are located in the outer third of her vaginal canal.

The glans of a man's penis has around 4,000 nerve endings with his frenulum and corona being very sensitive as well. Frenulum is the fold of skin right under the head of the penis on the underside of the shaft and the corona is the round border of the head of the penis, connecting it to the shaft on the belly side. The shaft and the scrotum are also rich in nerve endings and sensitive to pleasure.

All male and female genital structures have approximately the same number of nerve endings as they both start up as the same in the embryo. This deep sensitivity will be affected by any surgical procedure like circumcision or labiaplasty as any medical intervention will remove some of the nerve endings and will create scar tissue.

As we experience sexual arousal and orgasm, the brain is flooded with neurochemicals which create sensations of pleasure and emotions of love and attachment. Different areas of the brain keep receiving information from the body through the nervous system. As a result, the areas of the cortex responsible for reason and control shut down, and the area connected to pain is activated, explaining why there is a strong connection between pain and pleasure. There is also an activation in the amygdala which regulates emotions; in the areas responsible for dopamine release; in the cerebellum, which controls muscle function; and in the pituitary gland, which releases beta-endorphins, oxytocin and vasopressin. This means that different areas of the brain light up like a night sky during fireworks while others shut off.

As you are approaching the big-O, the hypothalamus and nucleus accumbens become activated and make your heart race, your skin flush, your pupils dilate and your breathing deepen. Oxytocin and dopamine flood your system, rewarding you with the ultimate pleasure response.

What follows is a post-orgasmic bliss where all the areas of the brain cool down and slowly return to a normal function. You feel high and the world feels amazing.

You do not need to know all the details of your anatomy of arousal. In fact, even scientists still struggle to fully understand the functioning of our brains. However, the more you know about your own body and what it likes, about different ways in which it responds to stimulation, the closer to God you can arrive yourself.

This is why masturbation is such an important activity in our sexual development. If you do not know your own body and your own pleasure map, you cannot successfully ask your lover to tease and please you.

Discovering your full orgasmic potential takes time, commitment and curiosity. We are all different and our bodies respond differently. Nobody has all the answers, but we can all learn from each other and enrich others with our own experiences.

I have learnt a lot through my own practice, but I still continuously learn from my clients and friends as they share with me their stories of self-pleasure, sexual unions, erotic experiences, multiple orgasms, pleasure, fun, playfulness, intimate bliss and also their struggles and frustrations. I doubt I will ever stop learning, which makes this journey even more exciting.

TWO BECOMING ONE

Do you remember Anthony, my skilled lover from Part 4? I want to bring him back here again because of a beautiful tantric practice we enjoyed together in bed. We were both very sensitive to the energy flowing between us and we played with it deliberately, which was sensually adding to our physical connection.

After a period of lovemaking, we would rest in each other's arms, with his lingam still inside me or not, and we would simply breathe together, feeling into the circle of energy flowing between our bodies. I particularly enjoy it when the breath is alternating between lovers. So as Anthony was inhaling I would exhale, and as he was exhaling I would inhale.

At the same time we were both visualizing that energetic flow between us. As I was inhaling, I was receiving his sexual energy flowing from his lingam into my yoni and then up to my heart. When I was exhaling, that flow was continuing from my heart into his and then down to his genitals.

As he was exhaling, he was sending the energy from his cock into my vagina, and on the inhale he was receiving energy from my heart into his. Maintaining the visualization and connected breath are particularly important at the beginning of the practice, but after a while you can let go and simply be. There is nothing else to do, nothing to control. It is time to be in your experience, flowing, sensing, enjoying. The energy will keep flowing so you can give in completely and surrender to the process.

I could just stay there for hours, sensing that flow, immersing myself in that circle of sexual energy, completely lost in this experience. The best word that comes to mind to describe it is "magic". Or "alternative reality". Or a "trance". The only times I ever get to experience these states is during sex – solo or partner sex. Or during a psychedelic journey.

Erotic trance

Erotic trance is a deeply embodied state of heightened awareness of all your bodily sensations. It is not a state of 'doing' but rather of 'being' in sex. This is a state where you are capable of experiencing not only greatly intensified pleasure and profound emotional states, but also visions, inspiration, wholeness, bliss and a strong clarity around your life.

The first step to arrive there is to learn to be fully present in our bodies. This can be challenging. In our culture we receive many negative messages about the body. The media and advertising are constantly telling us that we are not slim enough, not beautiful enough, not fit enough and that we are inadequate in a variety of ways, but as soon as we buy a certain product or service, we will be fine. This messaging, however, never ends and we never find ourselves fully satisfied. Poor body image is responsible for much disconnection that we experience in our society. Peer pressure adds to this situation, but the harshest critique of them all is that little nagging voice in our own heads.

There are also many people who experience trauma at some point of their lives and, as a result, they dissociate from their bodies in order to numb painful memories. Some traumatic events can cause us to hold chronic tension in our bodies, which reduces our ability to feel even further. Trauma can vary greatly from severe cases like rape or aggression to milder ones like unpleasant comments or uninvited advances. Trauma and dissociation can even come from such innocent behaviours as our parents cringing in disgust as they were changing our nappies. Their strong emotional reaction was sending an energetic message to the child saying that what happens between their legs is nasty, dirty or disgusting. This can lead to subconscious feelings of shame and guilt.

When we do not like our bodies, when we feel embarrassed about them, we do not want to feel them. And we cannot experience deep states of erotic trance if we are disconnected from our bodies in our everyday lives.

Exercise:

Try this exercise. Find a full-length mirror, preferably in your own home, and get fully undressed. Now look at your own body, really look at yourself, from your toes all the way up to the top of your head. What do you see? How do you feel about what you see? Are you looking at yourself with love? With compassion? With kindness? Or with embarrassment and shame? Can you even look at your own body?

Can you stand naked in front of your partner and ask them what they see? Ask them to describe your entire body, to describe their favourite features of your body. Observe closely all the emotions that arise. Are they positive or negative? Are you smiling, or do you feel embarrassed and annoyed?

Living in the body

Discovering a felt, lived reality of our bodies is, for many people, a life changing experience. It definitely was for me!

From our school days to our experience in modern society, we learn that thinking is superior to feeling; we learn to glorify and cultivate our minds at the expense of our bodies. But we are not heads on sticks. We have minds AND we have bodies. We think AND we feel. One cannot exist without the other. Ed Maupin's term "body epiphany" is a very personal realization of having a felt body – a body which is much more than just a physical object carrying the mind.

Once we wake up to this reality, there are many techniques that can help us develop a strong bond and connection with the body. As a starting point, it is extremely helpful to become sensitive and attuned to all the sensations, emotions and energy in the body. Being aware of one's breath and any areas of tension or relaxation. Taking mindful breaks throughout the day to just breathe and feel.

Aaaaah ...

ECO-SEX AND A SUN-GASM

I have an extremely soft spot in my heart for New Zealand. I have spent many beautiful, exciting or purely relaxing weekends there, surrounded by the magic of green hills, lush nature and serene beaches of breath-taking beauty. There is something very raw, ancient and sacred about that land, and it seduces my soul deeply every time I go there.

One spring, I was camping there with a group of friends. We would only visit urban areas to stock up on food and water. Other than that, we stayed immersed in wild areas, seeking remote locations and connecting with Mother Nature. New Zealand is abundant in gorgeous landscapes and every day was filled with awe, joy and tranquillity.

One morning I snuck out onto a nearby hill for my morning meditation. I sat down cross-legged on the grass, naked except for my undies, and I took a moment to admire my surroundings. It was warm and glorious. The sun was shining, the sky was blue and all I could see around were hills covered with green trees and bushes. The leaves were softly whispering in the gentle wind and the sun was kissing my skin. I closed my eyes and relaxed into a meditative state. Far away from the city, from work, from noise and long to-do lists, it was easy to let go of the world and just be.

I remained very present in my body, letting go of the mind but fully aware of my buttocks and legs resting on the grass, enjoying the warmth of the sun and the cooling breeze. I kept breathing consciously, taking in air in a full yet relaxed way. I felt like I was in a temple full of life and gentle sounds.

Through my eyelids I could still see the intense light of the sun. It was energizing me and refreshing me. The longer I was there, the more energized I felt with that beautiful, warm charge rising through my body. It felt like my body was a battery, slowly being filled up by the sunshine, from my legs all the way up to my head. The more lost in my experience I was, the more intense the energy felt in my body.

The experience culminated in an amazingly nourishing sun-gasm of orgasmic pleasure, warmth and sun energy exploding through my entire system.

Erotic connection with nature

Many people cultivate an erotic connection with Mother Earth. Nature is our true home and we have a natural connection to it beyond the artificial worldly possessions that we accumulate over our lifetimes.

Since ancient times people have been hugging trees, kissing plants, thrusting into the earth and massaging the ground with their feet. Meditating in nature has a completely different feel to it than doing it indoors.

Ecosexuality is a term that was promoted by Annie Sprinkle and Elizabeth Stephens, and it has existed since the early 2000s. Its expression varies from people who choose to use eco-friendly sex products to those who have deeply orgasmic experiences in rivers, waterfalls, forests and on the mountains. For many people this trend goes much deeper than pleasure and ecstatic moments. Most ecosexuals are committed to saving our environment and they see Earth not only as a lover, but as a lover in deep need of our awareness, help and loving kindness. We are living in a time of environmental crisis, and saving our planet will require a dramatic shift of consciousness.

Exercise

I would like to invite you to explore your own erotic connection with nature. Feel free to adjust this experience to your own comfort level, but do give it a go. It may be as simple as masturbating in your backyard or inhaling deeply the scent of the ocean. Caressing the sand or burying your face in the leaves. Allowing the waterfall to massage your naked body or offering your semen under the full moon.

Find your own very special place where you can make intimate contact with the Earth. Touch her, feel her, penetrate her, enjoy her. Tell her that you love her. Ask her what she needs and listen to her answers. Embrace her and allow her to embrace you.

Honour the Earth.

Do it alone or with a partner.

But do it!

LIVING AN ECSTATIC LIFE

As you might already be aware, it is a deeply enriching and exciting experience to take your sex life out of the bedroom and even out of your home. But there are many ways to do it other than having solo or partner sex out in nature. Some of those ways are more subtle or intense than others.

Barbara Carrellas is one of my biggest inspirations when it comes to having orgasmic experiences in all sorts of places and situations. Her book *Urban Tantra* is full of examples that will blow your mind! Listen to this:

"I've always subscribed to the theory that if you make love to the universe, the universe will make love to you, so I began using several of my favourite Tantric techniques to circulate sexual energy between me and Sydney. Nothing I was doing was obvious to anyone on the street; I'm sure I appeared to be nothing more than a smiling, happier-than-usual woman on her way to the post office. I had no big expectation of any particular climax as a result of my lovemaking with the city of Sydney. I most surely had no expectation of any particular physical sensation. But before I knew it, a little blissgasm shivered up my spine, followed by an actual clitoral orgasm that washed up the front of my body. These two waves crashed together in my head. I was so amazed, I had to stop and lean against a wall – I'd had a walking orgasm!"[12]

I'll have what she is having!

I am going to share with you one more story before I let you go. It is a story of my first ever heart-gasm. It happened at a kirtan event. Kirtan is an evening of music and chanting. The participants are led by the facilitator to sing lines of devotional text repeatedly, which has a quality of calming the mind and taking the person into a meditative state.

It did not take me long before I found myself completely immersed in the chant. The music was beautiful, the words were simple and it was extremely easy to follow along. There were around thirty of us in the room, singing in unison, and the space was vibrating powerfully with the strength of our voices.

There is an amazing power and quality to groups coming together to sing, dance, cheer, meditate, etc. The energy is multiplied so strongly, everybody can feel it, even if they have no idea what the energy is. It feels exhilarating, thrilling, exciting, joyful. This is why people love so much coming to sport events, even though it is so much cheaper and easier to watch the game on their TV at home. The energy of the crowd is so powerful, it is addictive.

At some point I realized that energy started to build up in the middle of my chest, in my heart centre. I was not certain what was happening but it felt very pleasant. It felt like tension, like someone was applying gentle pressure to my chest. I remained strongly aware of that area, enjoying the pleasure and feeling elated by it. I kept chanting with eyes closed; it was just me and the music. I felt calm yet energized by the sound.

The charge in my chest kept intensifying and it felt pleasant and warm. As the music started to speed up, the energy in the air became electric. I was completely lost in this experience, immersed in the chant, not a thought in my head. And then it happened …

The energy in my chest exploded with a great intensity, flooding my chest and then the rest of my body with a wave of hot, loving ecstasy. I opened my eyes and gasped in shock. Fortunately, I was already sitting down, otherwise I would have needed to lean on a wall as well!

What do you do after you have just orgasmed in a room full of people? I gave myself a few moments to process and integrate the experience and then I returned to chanting with a big smile on my face, excited to tell my friends all about it after the event was over.

Care for your body

As Eyal Matsliah points out in his book *Orgasm unleashed*: "When you expand your understanding of orgasm – your orgasm will expand"[13] and I completely agree. As long as you believe that all an orgasm is, is a series of sharp, pleasurable genital contractions following a period of arousal, that is the only kind of orgasm you will ever experience.

But once you open up your mind and your body to a wealth of new orgasmic explorations, your life will be enriched with bliss and pleasure wherever you turn. Our bodies can do amazing things, and in many cases all we need to do is simply surrender to our ecstatic energy. We are all ecstatic already, we simply trained ourselves to disconnect, dissociate and not feel our bodies, to live in our heads and neglect what happens from the neck down. Until one day something goes wrong and our bodies go to the extreme of using pain and discomfort in order to remind us about our physical aspect. Then we get scared, start to stress and worry, and look for outside solutions to 'fix' our body. But the body knows what it needs; it has a deep, inherent wisdom. And in many cases it is not tablets or outside intervention but simply to be cared for with more kindness and compassion.

In our modern society, we often abuse our bodies. We push ourselves to work harder, achieve more, spend longer hours at the computer desk. We use coffee to overcome natural energetic fluctuations of our body and we rely on packaged, highly processed foods or even fast foods. We ingest things that our bodies are not meant to take in, like dairy or processed sugars. Our bad habits have created cancer and many other diseases that our ancestors never had to deal with.

Taking care of your physical health is a very important aspect of an ecstatic life. The right diet and exercise routine are a great start to reconnecting with your body's needs. We are all unique, so you need to learn to listen to your own body in order to know what foods are best for you, how much water you need a day and whether you need to join the gym, go jogging or do yoga. Trial and error are a great system, so whenever you eat something, right after the meal and also two hours later, take note of how your body is feeling. Are you energized, satisfied, feeling light in your body or feeling heavy, sluggish and lethargic? Or maybe hungry again soon enough?

And when you exercise, try different workout routines, different intensities. Aches and pains might be there to alert you and ask you to take it easy. Or you might experience the kind of 'green pain' that is informing you that the body has just made an effort yet you are ready for more.

Are you a heavy user of alcohol, coffee, cigarettes or recreational drugs? How does your body feel after you use these substances? Past the initial high, do you need to recover each time? Are there side effects that you need to deal with? I once decided to quit alcohol for a year. It turned out to be much easier than I expected, and in addition I was saving money opting to drink water instead. And I was always able to drive myself home instead of having to look for taxis. And no hangovers – you have got to love that!

I do have an occasional glass of wine with dinner but when you only drink very little, one glass is plenty to satisfy you and I find that it is always enough for me. And I drink a coffee alternative made of chicory root – very yummy and very beneficial to your health!

Befriend your body

I would like you also to notice how you react when your body feels pain or discomfort. Most people tense up and respond with fear or irritation, immediately thinking about and analysing the best way to fix the problem. What I have learnt is to relax and lean into the pain, instead of trying to push it away. I embrace my pain and ask my body lovingly: "what is wrong?". In most cases, discomfort disappears and when it does stay, I am usually able to pinpoint its source and the best way to deal with it. I cannot remember the last time I had to take medication, and my body feels fantastic!

Whenever I encounter people who do not take care of their bodies, who keep complaining about their aches and pains, I usually recognize fairly quickly what is happening. Do your knees hurt? Your body might be telling you that you carry too much weight. Do you suffer from neck pain? It might mean that you sit at your computer desk too long and your body is alerting you of its need to move and stretch. You cannot run or perform any demanding physical activity because you keep finding yourself breathless? It might be time to quit cigarettes.

Make friends with your body. Do not see it only as a physical shell for your brain. It has a distinct ability to enrich your life experience through feeling and sensing. And when treated with the reverence that it deserves, it will offer you much more pleasure than pain!

Touch yourself lovingly and often, speak to your body with kindness. Treat your body as you would treat a small child. When a child is crying, we do not push it away and try to deny its existence. We embrace the child and hold it close, we comfort it and offer it help and support. We smile and say "it is going to be ok!". This is how I want you to see your body, as a beloved and cherished aspect of yourself.

I often stop and feel into my body. I take a few deep breaths and enjoy how it feels when the air is delightfully rushing into my system. I notice how relaxed my body is, or consciously let go of tension if there is any there. I correct my posture if I am sensing any discomfort. And I simply enjoy deep sensual awareness of my physical being. I find that the more I do it, the more delicious pleasure my body rewards me with.

FULL-BODY ORGASMS AND BEING
A MULTI-ORGASMIC MAN

There are two more final practices I want to leave you with. When I talk to my clients about having non-ejaculatory orgasms and being multi-orgasmic, they are usually surprised and ask whether this is even possible. Let me assure you that it is! I have trained hundreds of men in this technique and the feedback I receive is consistent and very inspiring: they have never experienced anything like that before in their entire lives and it is an experience much deeper, much more profound and ecstatic than any ejaculatory orgasm they have ever had.

This is the area of true tantric lover mastery, and a sure way to impress any woman in bed. There are some men for whom these practices are easy, natural and effortless. However, for most it takes training, patience and persistence to master them. The good news is that the techniques are not difficult and anybody can perform them. You do not need to have a certain body type or level of fitness, or even any spiritual awareness. If you have a male body, you are good to go!

237

I would like you to first commit to some preparatory training, and that involves strengthening your pelvic floor muscle. This is the muscle you use to stop the stream of pee, and you can find it easily by practicing in the toilet first. Once you are fairly aware of which muscle I am talking about, start exercising it whenever you are driving, watching TV, when you are at your computer or relaxing. All you need to do is squeeze the pelvic floor muscle (also known as the PC muscle) and then release it. Doing about a hundred squeezes per day will be a great start.

When you do your practice, remember that the release part is as important as the squeeze. In fact, it is a good idea to coordinate the squeeze with the breath: squeeze on the inhale and release on the exhale. As you are squeezing, do it firmly enough but without causing yourself any discomfort. And when you are releasing, make sure to relax the muscle completely before you start the next squeeze. If you keep squeezing without a full release, you might create quite a bit of tension in your genitals, which would not be comfortable or desirable.

Do not worry if you cannot hold your pelvic floor muscle tense for the entire duration of the inhale. This will come as the muscle becomes stronger. Do not worry either if you are squeezing not only that one muscle but also your anus, buttocks, lower belly and upper thighs. The more you practice, the better you will be able to isolate just that one area which is located between your anus and your scrotum, while the rest of your body will remain relaxed.

Once your PC muscle is fairly fit, you can start using it to train yourself to experience full-body, non-ejaculatory orgasmic states. These are highly erotic states where sexual energy remains in your body instead of being released out with the semen. This means that you can take your sex life into a completely new level where the ejaculation will seem like a genital sneeze as compared to deeply satisfying and nurturing states of expanded ecstasy that can last for hours.

The technique I am referring to is called The Big Draw in the tantric tradition.

Exercise:

You are going to start as usual, using touch, presence and deep breath to arouse your body. Take your time, do not rush the stimulation; you do not want to ejaculate, just to enter a state of sexual excitement and pleasure. Keep using deep breath to spread the delicious sensations all over your body. Keep playing with the edging technique to make yourself last much longer. Keep going for at least half an hour before you attempt to do the draw.

Once you are ready, start by taking about twenty or thirty fast breaths. Make sure that these are belly breaths and that your tummy is expanding and collapsing rapidly as you are breathing. After that, take two slow, deep breaths and on the third one, take in as much air as possible and hold it in for about fifteen seconds or longer – as long as it is comfortable for you to do so. As you are holding the breath, clench your PC muscle and push your entire body down into the mattress – push down your shoulders, arms, hands, buttocks, legs and feet.

Keep tensing up your entire body until you let go of the breath and exhale. Relax your body, keep your eyes closed and take a few minutes to enjoy and savour the ecstatic release happening inside of your body. You will experience shivers, tingles, pleasure, warmth, buzzing or vibrations, and aliveness spreading through your entire being. Some people start to shake ecstatically so if this happens, simply surrender and allow your erotic energy to move you. It is a very beautiful and deeply blissful experience. It will leave your body nurtured, energized and full of vitality. It is a fantastic way to start your day as that special buzz and virility will stay with you for many hours.

The Big Draw can happen in the middle of your intimate practice, either all by yourself or with a lover, or it can conclude it. With time, you can also start using it to take yourself into multi-orgasmic states. In order to do that, simply continue sexual stimulation after the draw; keep stroking your penis until you are ready for another full-body orgasm. With time and practice, your body will spontaneously start taking you into multiple full-body ecstatic states, even if you do not use the Big Draw anymore. This technique is simply a training tool for your body, teaching it to move and expand your erotic energy beyond your genitals and with time – beyond your body, connecting you with the entire Universe and all the beings in it.

Practice makes perfect

Your sexual energy is sacred – it is your life force. The more you revere and respect it, the more it will serve you. The more you waste it, the more depleted your body will become. Retaining that erotic charge within the body has multiple benefits and offers you a world of experiences not known to most of the men in our modern society.

Please be aware, however, that the body needs time to learn and to adjust to new practices and new ways of playing with sexual energy. It is not likely that you will experience a huge difference from one day to the next, but the patience and dedication will definitely pay off. Your full-body orgasms might, at the beginning, feel fairly gentle compared to ejaculation. This is because the sexual energy is expanding over a larger surface of your body instead of staying localized just in your genitals. But as you practice, each time you will reach a deeper and deeper state of pleasure and orgasmic ecstasy. Each time you will lose yourself a little more in your experience until one day your entire body will feel the way your genitals feel during ejaculation now. You will feel absolutely no need to release as you will reach a highly erotic state with your entire body buzzing and vibrating in intense ecstasy. You will feel energized, rejuvenated, nourished and satisfied.

There is absolutely no comparison between an expanded ecstatic experience and a release-style orgasm. On top of charging and nurturing the body, these high erotic states also nurture your mind and soul. Many men speak of spiritual or mystical experiences as they dance on the wave of a prolonged orgasmic state which can go on for hours. Please remember, however, that every intensity and length of an erotic state is perfect and beautiful. Do not discard the milder ones in a chase of the big ones. Savour and cherish them all!

Dry orgasms

The second technique I want to teach you is an alternative way to enjoy non-ejaculatory orgasms. Here you will make a different use of your PC muscle. Let me explain.

Men are usually not capable of peeing and ejaculating at the same time. This is caused by the tension in the pelvic floor muscle which shuts down your ability to urinate as you are becoming more and more aroused. In this practice, I want you to remain very aware of your PC muscle. Preferably you have been strengthening it for a while now and you know exactly where it is. It will help tremendously if you can tense and relax it at will.

Exercise:

Start as usual, stimulating your sexual energy and arousing yourself in any way that you like. Keep going for as long as you wish, playing with different techniques you learnt in this book, or any techniques that you prefer.

As soon as you find yourself close to ejaculation, consciously relax the PC muscle. This will signal to your body that you want to urinate and the ejaculation process will be blocked. As you remain relaxed and keep stimulating your arousal, you will most likely trick your body to taking you into an orgasmic state even though there is no ejaculation. It might take some time to master this technique so do not become discouraged if you do not succeed the first few times.

Once you get a hang of this, it will become easier and easier to trigger deep states of ecstasy at will. Many people accidentally experience these states once or twice in their lives, but then have no idea how to go back there. The techniques described here will help you reach intense orgasmic bliss whenever you want. And the fun part is that after each orgasm you can keep going as there will be no refractory period, and you can resume sexual stimulation if you want to!

PUTTING IT ALL TOGETHER

In this last part we have ventured beyond what most people would normally classify as sex, or would ever include in their sex routine. But you are here because you want to know more, you want to learn what else is possible, right?

Many people come to me for sex coaching and say: "I just know that there is more ...". If this resonates with you, rest assured that a lot of people feel the same way. We have a deep yearning for something really true and profound and we intuitively know that it is possible, even if we are not certain how to get there.

Whether you just want really, really good sex, or you want to connect your spirituality with your sexual practice, or you want to see and feel your partner in a way nobody has ever seen them before, you can achieve all that and more. You just need a curious mind, a good teacher and a commitment to practice.

So to recap what we have learnt here:

1/ Keep exploring new sex skills – reading, researching and studying them – and then take action and practice, practice, practice. That is the only way to actually make a difference in your sex life!

2/ Start by practicing on your own first, before you bring a new skill to your partner. It takes time to build your level of confidence with a new practice, so be patient and gentle with yourself.

3/ Practice embodiment. Do the mirror exercise: look at your own naked body with love, compassion and delight. What are you noticing?

4/ Once you are ready, invite your partner to practice with you. Explain to them what you want to achieve and set an intention for your lovemaking.

5/ Explore nature as a lover. Create your own eco-sexual experience. Find the right place, the right time and the right way to make love to the Earth.

6/ Look at your definition of orgasm – is it serving you or limiting you? How can you expand it in order to live an ecstatic life, not just in the bedroom but every moment of your day?

7/ Experiment with full-body orgasms, dry orgasms and being a multi-orgasmic man. Let go of your attachment to ejaculation and explore what else is possible.

The feedback I consistently receive from my clients is that they are deeply grateful and very excited by all the new possibilities that they learn about from me. They finally get to ask all the questions they might have had about sex all their lives, and they are given a permission to learn, enjoy and explore freely.

To feel fully accepted and supported in your individual sexual expression is an amazing gift for anybody. Are you currently receiving that in your life?

Is it time you joined the ride?

CONCLUSION

So there you have it – a journey from frustration to bliss, from pain and shame to orgasmic ecstasy. I came a long way from being raised in a Catholic family – in a society that suppresses sex and its healthy expression – to embracing my erotic self and to awakening my sexual goddess within.

I am very passionate about helping others on their own sexual path. I believe that sex and pleasure are our birthright and I happily get involved in any projects or initiatives that support this goal. I have a vision of a new society where sex is embraced as a very healthy and natural aspect of our beings. I believe that Tantra can become a new yoga, with people of every gender, age, race and belief system coming together to study this ancient art of intimate connection.

I want to see a new culture where we teach our teenagers about building a real sexual union, about consent, boundaries, respect and about states of profound embodiment instead of disconnection and dissociation. I want young people to have an alternative source of a meaningful sexual education so they do not need to learn from pornographic videos.

I want all of us to develop a healthy and natural connection to our sexuality so that we can become whole again. Sex is a part of us; in fact, we all come into this world through sex. It is time to let go of the stigma and taboo around it. It is time to embrace it and to celebrate it.

And how is your connection to your own body, to your sex and to your lover? Where are you at on your sexual journey? Are you happy, fulfilled and nurtured by your sexual connections? Or are you looking for more?

I hope that this book has opened your eyes to new possibilities and that you learned a thing or two. And if you are ready to really take a plunge, get in touch with me about my Legendary Lover coaching sessions. Please also feel free to send any feedback, comments or questions.

You can reach me through my website: www.helenanista.com.au or through my Facebook page: https://www.facebook.com/helenanista/.

Make sure to subscribe to my newsletter to hear all my news. It is packed with yummy sex tips and advice. And you can also take a fun quiz on my page, to find out what kind of a lover you are and where you can improve your skills for more pleasure, connection and playfulness in the bedroom.

And lastly, the journey of sexual awakening never ends. Mine has been quite a ride so far but I am still far from coming to any form of an end. I do not actually believe there is such a thing as an 'end' when it comes to our sexual potential. I am sure there are still many kinds of orgasm I have not experienced yet and so many more mind-blowing intimate encounters that I will have. Again and again I keep enjoying what I can only describe as the best sex of my life ... so far. And I wish you the same.

So here it is: to the best sex of your life ... again and again, and again!

ABOUT THE AUTHOR

Helena Nista is a sexpert and Tantra teacher. She has a wealth of experience working with men, women and couples. She works best with corporate, middle-aged men who want to be better lovers. Her ideal clients are curious by nature and want to explore alternative ways of having longer lasting sex and being amazing lovers.

She is a certified sexologist, a certified Tantra practitioner and has worked with over 1,000 clients in the past three years, with over 90% of them reporting a dramatic improvement in their sex lives.

Helena teaches her clients beautiful tools and rituals of tantric love-making. She shows them how to develop a much deeper and more profound connection with their partners. She helps them obtain much more sexual satisfaction, pleasure and nurturing in their relationships.

She created a unique program, Legendary Lover, that she delivers as a keynote speech, a workshop and one-on-one sessions.

Helena's clients come to her because they are bored or frustrated with their sex lives. Many just know that there must be more to sex and they want to reach that deeper level. What people learn about sex in our modern world is very limited. We have an inner knowledge that much more is possible, yet nobody tells us how to get there. What we see on TV and the internet is barely scratching the surface of our sexual potential, and the porn industry is not helping either.

The problems Helena's clients usually struggle with are: sexual boredom and frustration, premature ejaculation or erectile difficulty, porn addiction, performance anxiety or difficulty orgasming and a desire to reach a new, exciting depth and satisfaction in their relationships.

Her second mission in life is being a mum to a gorgeous little cat who brings much joy, love and cuddles into her life. She is both guilty and proud of taking countless photos of Rosie and posting them on social media. In her spare time she loves to escape the city and spend time in nature, going for walks and meditating.

You can visit her website www.helenanista.com.au and take her unique quiz – What Kind of Lover Are You?

Make sure to check out her coaching programs for more sexual pleasure, connection, satisfaction and playfulness. You can also follow her on Facebook and Instagram for fresh, fun, juicy ideas and tips about intimacy.

CONTACT HELENA
Website: www. helenanista.com.au
Email: helena@helenanista.com.au
Phone: +61 405 136 505
Social media handles: @helenanista

ENDNOTES

1. R. Louis Schultz, PhD, *Out in the Open, The Complete Male Pelvis*, North Atlantic Books, 2012, 28-29.

2. Jack Morin, PhD, *The Erotic Mind, Unlocking the Inner Sources of Sexual Passion and Fulfillment*, HarperCollins Publishers, 1995, 139-168.

3. Chantelle Boscarello (Raven) and Simon Martin, *Song of Tantra, A Manual for Tantric Relationship*, Eliyah, 33.

4. Edward W. Maupin, PhD, 'Somatic Education: its Origins, Ancestors, and Prospects', http://www.edmaupin.com/Somatic_Origins.html, 1998.

5. Lizette Borreli, 'National Orgasm Day 2014: Common Myths About the Female Orgasm (You Probably Believe)', http://www.medicaldaily.com/national-orgasm-day-2014-6-common-myths-about-female-orgasm-you-probably-believe-295906, 2014.

6. Barbara Carrellas, *Urban Tantra, sacred sex for the twenty-first century*, Celestial Arts, 2007.

7. Barbara Carrellas, *Urban Tantra, sacred sex for the twenty-first century*, Celestial Arts, 2007, 29.

8. Barbara Carrellas, *Urban Tantra, sacred sex for the twenty-first century*, Celestial Arts, 2007, 98-108.

9. The School of Life, 'Why You Shouldn't Trust Your Feelings', The School of Life, 2016, https://www.youtube.com/watch?v=nZYzzn6W2qc&t=17s.

10. Dr. Betty Martin, 'Wheel of consent', http://bettymartin.org/category/wheel-of-consent/.

11. David Deida, *The Way of the Superior Man, A Spiritual Guide to Mastering the Challenges of Women, Work, and Sexual Desire*, Sounds True, 2004, 87-88.

12. Barbara Carrellas, *Urban Tantra, sacred sex for the twenty-first century*, Celestial Arts, 2007, 84.

13. Eyal Matsliah, *Orgasm Unleashed, Your guide to pleasure, healing and power*, Intimate Power, 2015, 13.

Made in United States
Troutdale, OR
11/22/2024

25161960R00146